First printing, March, 2019.

Cover Art, *Held Together*, by Laura Hohlwein. Used with permission.

Section Photography by Peter Spencer.

Cover & Book Design by Bodhi.

ISBN: 978-0-9996247-8-4

Library Of Congress Control Number: 2019933074

A Lake House Publication

Cold River Press
15098 Lime Kiln Road
Grass Valley, CA 95949
www.coldriverpress.com

This book is dedicated to our families, friends, those ships in the night that will always remain with us, and Annie....you are always in our hearts, every day.

For Nate —
Brilliant artist, thinker,
& soul. You mean so
much to me & Fred.
We treasure your friendship.

Love,
Victoria
5-23-2019

TOUGH ENOUGH
Poems From The Tough Old Broads

MENEBROKER ❖ DALKEY
WEINBERG ❖ HOHLWEIN

FOREWORD

As you will discover in this book there is a lot of history with the Tough Old Broads. There is the history between them, the history of their poetry together in Sacramento and the history of being "Tough Old Broads". But there is also a far greater history that they share; the history of poetry in Sacramento and the intertwined roles these four women played in the development of that poetry over the last fifty plus years.

It was through Ben Hiatt that I first met Ann Menebroker. Annie was working with Ben and Joyce Odam publishing various titles. I had known of Ann's work from the Wormwood Review and other little magazines around the country and found her to be "the real deal" when it came to poetry. Ann's work was straight forward no holds barred beautiful poetry that spoke directly to the heart and soul. I was captivated by her work early on and over the years became a great fan of her work. Ann didn't read often but when she did it was always worth any effort to hear her recite. Ben and I both championed her work. Hiatt loved working with these two women and I felt like I had come to the right place, being able to work in the same city as these fine poets.

I had obtained permission to publish poetry out of the Art Department at CSU Sacramento (Sacramento State College at the time) and met a graduate student in printmaking there, Fred Dalkey and his wife Victoria. We eventually created a mimeograph magazine with Ingrid Swanberg called "My Landlord must be Really Upset". It featured work by all four of us and other local and national poets. It only ran a couple of issues but it was the beginning of Victoria's outstanding poetry and the start of her writing in earnest. Even Fred, who is a visual artist, contrasted a verse or two. Victoria hit the ground running and her poetry remains of the first water, clear, incisive and always beautiful.

Working at Sacramento State I continued to meet a number of other poets, Kathryn Hohlwein, and Viola Weinberg among them. Kathryn was teaching at Sacramento State in the 1960s. Her husband, Hans, was Fred Dalkey's graduate advisor and I met Kathryn through Hans, Fred, and Victoria. Kathryn was, and is, the most gracious and eloquent of poets. I was completely charmed by her and have treasured her friendship and the quality of her poetry ever since. Her work with Homeric verse is outstanding and her own poetry is remarkable, chatting with her audiences whenever she reads developing a close kinship with her listeners as she reads.

I have a very long history with Viola Weinberg and have been close to her since before she published her first book. She has always been an exquisite poet. We worked together in many circumstances,, some literary, some not. She was news director at KZAP radio when I had a program on the station called Art Flash, teaching me how to run the broadcast board and mentoring me in radio. Later, when I ran the art component for CETA (Comprehensive Employment and Training Act) for the State of California, I hired Viola and we often read together. She became the editor of Inside Art (the gallery newsletter), hosted poetry readings, handled art and hung shows. Her work is stunningly beautiful and we have stayed very close over the years.

These incredible souls claim that I am a commonality among them, asking me to pen this Foreword because of it. I could not be prouder of that connection. Since the 1960's I have worked with these four Tough Old Broads and have loved their work. To know these women and to have interacted with them for the past fifty plus years has been, in a word, wonderful. In the time that I have known and worked with them, Sacramento has become a major poetry center on the West Coast. It is in large part because of these Tough Old Broads that this is so. They are strong, talented and excellent poets. They are lights of the Western Sierra and they are the pride of Sacramento, instrumental in so many ways to the developing poetry scene that was Sacramento in the '60s, 70's and on to today.

In writing this Foreword I decided to let this be a brief history of Ann's, Victoria's, Kathryn's and Viola's contribution to Sacramento and poetry in general, rather than speak to their individual poetries. They have been lights in my heart and their work has sustained me since I arrived in this city over fifty years ago. The work in this collection is why I stayed in Sacramento and continue to do so. We are fortunate to have these Tough Old Broads that did so much for poetry in our region, here in this book you are holding. Sadly, Ann Menebroker did not live to see this book, succumbing to cancer in 2016. In a fitting testament to how powerful her influence was in Sacramento and how the irony of life plays out daily, Dave Boles, publisher of Cold River Press (the publisher of this book), revealed to me that if it were not for Ann's encouragement and support he would have ceased publishing long ago. That is but one of many examples of how these "Tough Old Broads", individually and collectively, shaped the poetry experience that is Sacramento poetry today.

I love them very much and hold them dear. I know you will as well.

D.R. Wagner
January, 2019

TOUGH
ENOUGH

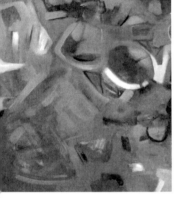

MENEBROKER

HOHLWEIN

DALKEY

WEINBERG

THE STORY OF THE TOUGH OLD BROADS

I'm a tough old broad from Brooklyn. Don't try to make me into something I'm not. If you want someone to tiptoe down the Barkley staircase in crinoline and politely ask where the cattle went, get another girl.
Barbara Stanwyck

There are millions of tough old broads. But there were always four of us; the Tough Old Broads. Our domain: poetry. Between us, there are many years of living with the throttle wide open, preferring to live life to the fullest over safe existences on the 'Barkley staircase' of comfortable life in boring, safe, and unremarkable situations. The TOBs, as we call ourselves, are not the type to play it safe.

We feel strongly about things. We fearlessly fell in love, and became writers

Somewhere along the second half of the last century, feminists began to see "broad" as a pejorative. Like "chick" or "bitch," broad became a slang term, referring to a woman who had seen it all. These are terms eschewed by early feminism.

Eventually, women took back tough old broads, as a spirited, sometimes saucy, and perhaps cantankerous moniker. Broad was originally hipster talk, jazz talk, for the female counterparts of 'cats' and 'dudes.' The Urban Dictionary explains it as slang for female, being broader than a male in the hips. Later, a noir quality of some women to meet, match and raise any man's toughness resonated with detective writers who coined the term tough old broad to describe a woman who has witnessed terrible things, used her ferociousness to defend herself against any threat, or to withstand life's awful blows.

These things were on my mind when the idea of banding together with Annie Menebroker, Kathryn Hohlwein and Victoria Dalkey popped into my head one day while writing a poem. Just a year before, I had lost my intense and accomplished daughter to a suicide. For almost a year, I sat in the garden, numb as a stone. The grief was, indeed, too much to bear.

During this time, I reached out to my close friend, Annie. She thought it might be good for me to talk to Kathryn. Kathryn is the founder of The International Readers of Homer, a nonprofit that hosts readings of Homer's epics all over the world. She had lost a vibrant daughter just months before. She understood tragedy at the highest level.

I don't remember much about that call, but I do remember that Kathryn and I sobbed rather loudly, keening hard, incredulous at the nerve of death to take the beautiful young women we so adored. Somewhere in that clothes-rending, chest heaving moment, a kernel was formed. In our hour of grief, we understood each other at a molecular level. I asked her, "How did you survive?" She answered with a woofing gasp, "You just go on."

And you write.

There would be more tears. When Annie said she was diagnosed with incurable liver cancer, I was so shocked that I ordered us both a glass of wine—disregarding her diagnosis. I realized that my precious friend would not be eternal, one of the most disturbing thoughts I ever had. I went home and cried so hard the dog started barking and wouldn't stop.

And you treat every moment together like a citadel.

Time passed. One day, I accompanied my husband to Sacramento. He was on a business trip, and I decided to take a water exercise class at the Sacramento YMCA. One exercise involved dividing up the swimmers and having them paddle toward each other to the other side. As I did, I couldn't believe my eyes. There, paddling along toward me was Victoria Dalkey!

Our children had grown up together, in the same elementary classes. We had known each other through Sacramento's life in the arts. Victoria, or V2 as I affectionately call her, has the most beautiful voice, cool and soft as water flowing over sand. She is also the longtime arts reviewer for the Sacramento Bee. She told me that she, too had fought cancer since we had last seen each other. We renewed our friendship, and it stayed with me like a small beating heart.

A few weeks later, Stage Four Cancer nearly claimed me as its victim. I collapsed with a shattered femur. They gave me a few months to live. I fought like a Hell cat, and I'm still here. I've been through many operations, enough radiation to leave my leg smoldering with heat, and years of physical therapy. During this time, I was called a Tough Old Broad by any number of people. I liked it. I started to write again, and the faces of my beloved friends appeared over and over to me.

Annie said we should get together. I said, "Let's do a reading." The following year, we pulled together for a magical, warm afternoon with about 300 people in attendance, sponsored by the Sacramento Poetry Center. It was the most dazzling experience any of us had ever had with poetry.

People seemed to relate to our joy. Not perfect, but so happy to be alive. We are who we are, and we were satisfied and happy to be Tough Old Broads, who had endured so much to laugh at the troubles we had fought so hard.

Soon after this enormous reading, I brought up the idea of this book.

Timing is everything, and all of us were tired. Annie was especially tired, and it became clear that she was not the same woman who bounced up the stairs at our reading to holler, "You can call me Annie!" We lost dear Annie the following year.

I never put the idea to bed, and was deliriously happy when D.R. Wagner, a friend of all the TOBs, suggested Cold River Press as a home for a collection of our work. After speaking with Cold River's publisher, Dave Boles, and caucusing with the remaining TOBs and Annie's daughter, Sue Menebroker McElligott, the idea began to take form as the book you hold in your hands. About thirty poems each, this book catalogs our book of hours, each poem a thousand years in the making, or a New York minute of insight.

So, forget that old Barkley staircase, and come with us. Life, so dear, is meant to be lived. We welcome you all.

Viola Weinberg

TABLE OF CONTENTS

ANNIE MENEBROKER

TABLE OF CONTENTS

KATHRYN HOHLWEIN

TABLE OF CONTENTS

VICTORIA DALKEY

TABLE OF CONTENTS

VIOLA WEINBERG

ANNIE MENEBROKER

Eighty years was simply not enough for Ann Menebroker. Known affectionately as Annie, she was a poet of international standing. Writing from the 1950s to her death in 2016, Menebroker published over 20 books of poetry and was heavily anthologized. Her work appeared in many small press magazines and poetry journals. She was enamored of poetry and poets, fascinated by people, and fully engaged in life. Her friendships were legion, and famously epistolary. Annie was known as one of the few women involved in the "no apologies school of Meat Poetry," writing with a clarity of emotion that enveloped the reader into her world of raw reality. In one moment her poetry is soft and inviting, in the next she exposes a world that is shackled by its heartlessness. No sense of illusion with her writing; only honesty and a purity of word play that resonates with us all.

THE WORDS DUMP OVER

The side of a table
marooned in a small
apartment. There they
lie, waiting for the
vacuum of hope
to sweep them
out of sight.
Only a tiny light
shines from the
machine's forehead.
The last time I stepped
on fallen words
they broke the skin's
surface.

IN ALL DIRECTIONS

As honestly as I can say it,
I think love
is about as important
as the air
that goes into our lungs.
I think that when
we can't love,
the heart gets
a muddier sound to it
and then the air
makes a lot of noise
like a fan, with maybe
a piece of paper caught in it,
whirling around,
making uneven paths
of wine
in our lives,
tossing our hair around
in all directions
even if we've just
fixed it
to look our best.

DAFFODILS AND HUNTER THOMPSON

(for Meade Fischer)

When i'm 90 i'll go live
in a dumpster and wear
old pieces of flags.

i'll roar when i can
and piss on the walls
of garbage that have
become home.

Visions of Hunter
Thompson will dance
in my dreams and songs
he sang will spill
into my mouth.

Wine and words
and life will be my
backdrop in this
immense theater
where art and craft
define my being
along with surfboards
and mountains
and a young
group of
yellow daffodils
that pronounce
beauty in spite
of us.

COMPOSITION

illness is such a distraction, so he puts
headphones on and listens to music
which is also a way to get to go to other
places.
his dentist has offered it as well as his
surgeon. when he takes the one he loves
into his arms there is music, but also
through its osmosis, a giving back
of the delectable and perceived beat
and the measure of small gratitudes.

CHROME POEM

There is this life, too
the one without explanations
where fortunes of butterflies
are released out into the fields
and not stuck to a collection board
not held by pins and explanations

Noah's Ark
rising from wood and ashes;
the kingdom of kingdoms.
What animals will you have?
Pair me off with fish or foul or beast.
If you are poor, I will come in a poor car.
If you are rich, I will come in a rich car.
If you are dead, I will come in a hearse.
If you are creative, I will vanish.

Farewell to emptiness and machines,
love-boys piled high, waiting for me.
Farewell to problems and blessings,
a network of systems in their dark keeping.

Butterflies stumble from field to field
erecting death by sexual stimulations
with the flowers.

(O laugh at my presumptions)
Noah, you bastard! Freaking out with the animals.
That was no dove you saw – it was a butterfly!
It could not possibly have brought you part of a
tree.
You were your own liberation, you fool!

Butterfly
Butterfly
peeing in the garden
without the sun
to turn you gold.
The darkness,
the turning, the turning.

CRAVINGS

Been wanting to see the ocean
for nine years.
It's a short drive from the city
where I live.

I used to write a lot of poems
about the ocean.
Suicide poems.
Love poems.
Death and sex poems.

In all of them I could feel
the wind coming off the bay
and smell that wet tug of waves
rolling over onto the shore.

The closest piece of ocean
in nearly one hundred miles
from where I live, traveling west.

I guess it's still there.

Last time I got within walking distance
I was in a car and my friend said,
"It's that way," and pointed.
"But we don't have time to go there."

I could smell it.
But I never saw it.

You have to have a raw
imagination, and a craving
so deep, you could get
lost remembering.

I dance under the valley of the moon.
I dance under the valley of the shore.
I dance under the valley of the ocean.
I dance under the valley of the breeze.

I dance over reluctant waves.
I dance over reluctant fish.
I dance over reluctant memories.
I dance over the smell of seaweed.

Come into my arms.
Come into my dreams.
Come into my weather.
Come into my strange world.

This is the valley, not an ocean.
Don't tell anyone.
Goddamnit, don't tell anyone.

EDDIE IS A DOLL SOMEONE SEWED TOGETHER

Eddie is in his round bottom canoe
going down the American river.
It's dangerous.
All he has for an oar
is some sort of short-handled broom.
Water sweeps through the bristles
effortlessly.
He thinks he has some control.
He sits up in his canoe
like the captain of a ship
thinking he can make sense
of this journey, do something
about the direction.
What he doesn't grasp
is, Eddie isn't even real.
He has no spirit, no origin.
He has no background,
no parents, no one to love him.
Everything about him
has been made up.
But he just might make it anyway.

HER NAME WAS HELEN

My philosophy professor, who taught ethics, died very old but not of natural causes. She was run over by a truck in a Target parking lot, probably with a red and white plastic bag near her body, and no one to claim her.

She was not very tall, but sometimes I felt it would be easier to bring a ladder to class to look up to her level of grace.

WHAT IT IS TO BE A "MEAT POET"
(for Ronald Baatz)

"Cold as the end of the world here," he wrote
and because everything I hear or see becomes
meat for poetry, I throw it in the pot, see
what kind of stew it'll make, what flavor
it might add. So many phrases, lines
from old songs, images of other experiences
come up, that it's as if the thief in me
has come alive, picking the lock
of every brain with a thought. If I
bang on your window at some weird
hour, for christsakes, don't open
the door!

IN THE RIVER TOWN OF LOCKE

the intersections have no street lights
just fences, mostly white picket
and flowers and trees.
It's very narrow, the town.
If you had the long arms of dreams
you could touch both sides.
If I had the nerve of spring, I could
touch your heart in ways
you never imagined, just me
with my magic love, on these
cracked sidewalks. We could
sit in the ancient free standing
bathtub, left in an alley, washing one
another, careful not to let anything
empty down the drain.

IN THE SOFT LIGHT OF BEING

for Samuel Charters

This is where the wind blows
curtains billowing
for attention, the room holding
bed and table, lamp and chair
books and photographs.
His darling wife
turning a page.
Imagine a rowboat oar
floating, the figure in the bed
rolling over like a wave, to touch
the air, swimming
through it, arm over
arm, the pillow falling
to the floor, the ocean gone silent.

LOVE

what i know about love
could fill a bottle cap.
but sometimes i
use the word because
it feels good
and right to do so.
if we wait to express
something until we fully
understand it, we would
stand around like they
did in the depression
waiting for apples or jobs.

MUSIC AND LIFE ON THE RIVER

This river moves so slowly it never seems to
go anywhere at all. It's not as if anyone can find
inspiration here, yet, if someone loves you
like this river moves, you don't have to
impress or speak in tongues.
It's a slow, melodious song backed up by
the sweep and wind through sticks and leaves.
The standard here is long-lasting. Nothing gets
lost that can't be found again, and the
fish grow fat from handouts. Dead critters
on shore turn to instant beauty. They
have left their bones to form art
in layers of dirt and moss. I saw a man
playing a violin, sitting in a tree branch. It
was foggy and he kept having to tune
the strings. This river, if you listen,
sings a song on its journey. And the song
ends up maybe in Mexico or Brazil.
And the river pretends it doesn't know
anything about the journey. But it's
all there.

OLD TIMES

When I was very young
there was a terrible war
and lots of people died.
I didn't understand too much.
I went to school and loved
to mix the orange powder
into the white margarine.
My family was scattered.
My parents divorced.
And when the war was over
I remember bells ringing
everywhere. I knew I was
supposed to be happy, so
I smiled and said, "Hurrah!"
And Mama said we should be
grateful, and I tried to be.

PORTRAIT AT DUSK
For my grandchildren

There are times
when you wake up to grief.
A hammer slams
in the side
of an old house, brings
it down; the rubble
is hauled away
as if it never existed.

The new building goes up, all sleek,
chrome and glass.
You wonder
where the spirit of the building
will reside.
Spirits live in warm places.

There are times when you look up
and the sky is so dirty
it looks like a storm
is moving in.

REMEMBER RITA HAYWORTH

remember rita hayworth
the dazzle of her long, red hair
slinking onto the screen
singing love songs
her body gyrating from the hips
down, and some man ringside
cigarette in his mouth
watching her as if he owned her.

in the same film someone always
gets murdered, rita is always
blamed and gets shot in her
fabulous chest, crumbling so beautifully
(or really, kind of sliding) to the floor
not a hair out of place, making death
seem classy.

SINGING MADMEN

7:30 a.m.
a powerful time to get up
or go, finally, to bed
or listen to others doing it.
As long as it isn't Sunday
we have a chance.

The clock, looking like a gunner
ready for battle
points its bullets
and Z I N G !
Ah…I've been plugged again
by TIME and oatmeal
and a scuffle outside my door.

Maybe it's the morning paper
or the milkman
or some drunk
looking for a door to sag on.

Here in this room
I prefer silence
without news or eggs
or even the poor sad drunk.

There is a spider above the ceiling
named Kafka.
We have an understanding
not to bother one another.
But there are times
when just for the evil of it
I would like to smash him down
without warning.

I think he knows this
for he never sleeps.
And this is the way we live
(all of us)
waiting for our chance
with eyes open
still clogged
with yesterday's images.

Waiting like little boys
in closets
or girls in love
or singing madmen
to test our skills
against the best
and find it has been
the least of our glories.

7:30 a.m. and the drunk
sinks farther down the door.
I will bring him in
with the paper, the milk
and eggs
and he will babble some
early gratitude
to which I reply:

"Livingstone, I presume?"

SINGING THE BEAR OUT OF THE WOODS

A bear is too big to dance
on points
or wear tutus

A bear roars
and tall trees sway

A bear lumbers towards you
on all fours
and you run record fast
knowing there's no way
you can win the race.

A bear meets up with a poet
who shows his heart
beating in his chest
thump-ta-thump-ta-thump
and the sound
mesmerizes him into stillness

The poet isn't stupid enough
not to have fear
but his song
is in the right place

The bear and the poet
dance to the inner music
in a slow circle
of respect

The bear only came of out the woods
to hunt for berries

The poet came out of the night
to dream under the sun.

SOMETHING ABOUT FLYING PIGS

The sky is so impersonal.
You see that holy man who trips
over his thoughts? Listen, why do
you parade through this
heart without music? Tell me this:
is poetry enlarged by experience
or love? Humor is at least
patriotic. My toes are smiles
and I'm not an antidote for
your bad days.

THE BLUE FISH

It is not
the conservative life
that stifles, but the someone
who offers to share it
with you, endorses it,
propagates it.
Somewhere inside of me
this tiny blue fish
swims. It
bumps against my quiet.
Its little mouth
opens and shuts
like a busy
supermarket door.
It has no entrails.
It is just this
tiny blue body
floating inside of me,
making an impression
like braille.
I try to find
food for it
with words. It swims
into my brain
and in the night, I have
a blue orgasm.

THE BULL THAT DIED IN THE RAIN

He came to me in a dream
holding a light
and beckoning

Because I dreamed, there was
no danger, and I followed.

He showed me an eternity
of dreamers
masturbating on death, whose
desires were finished.

In the night of my learning
there came a hunger. When I woke,
the dream was slowly digesting

and the plenty of my being
began to eat the bed.

"THE COMMON SMILE OF UNTHINKING HAPPINESS"
Gao Xingjian, *"Soul Mountain"*

In Marin County, there
was a Sleepy Hollow Road.
I was too young
to know about the headless
horseman, the wild tale
of darkness and fear.
That was to come later.
I dared myself to jump
off the high dive board
at the community pool.
I kissed a boy named
Tommy Preston that everyone
said came from a bad
family. Then I moved away
but took Tommy with me
where he remains some
fifty years later, judged
because he was poor —
but not by me.

THE MECHANICS OF
WHAT STIRS
for Ken Kirby

I am the last poem
you will hear.
Every part of this day
sings in me.
All of the music
comes through
to reach and move us.
My words hold you
closer than blankets.
All of the downtown
people smile at us.
We smile back.
They know.
And yes, I like
your new pearls
and your old you.

THE OLDEST PROFESSION (LOVE)

I love
so much
that i
am either
the world's
biggest whore
or its greatest saint

THE POEM THAT WAS MAGNIFICENT

came over email, came like the earth
shaking around you, came like a flood
of beautiful language. It could never
be a haiku, or close to a tanka;
it would be Mt. Kilimanjaro
in Tanzania. It would be adjectives
and gospel truth. It would be
deep river honesty. It would
be the mosquito and the leopard.
It would sting. It would eat
flesh. It would sing arias
and balance twelve moons.
It would be valet service
to your first appetite. It would
make you not want to be a
poet anymore, but to be
the poet's material. It would
be like the first time your
child came to you and
called you its own country.

THIS

you get out of bed
solemnly naked
and lumber somewhere out of sight.
the house is a mystery
the way it swallows
whoever leaves warm sheets.
lying here
in my own bare skin
I think how I love the sight
of unclothed people
going about the business of love.
everything else is so ruined.
the room. the world. the landscape.
the way to stay beautiful
is to avoid mirrors
and look only at those
who truly love back.

Tulare Motel

Sometimes if summer couldn't
get over itself, Wilma would take
her August body to a motel
for a couple of days where air
conditioning was another sweet
revival. Her apartment was left
to take up the slack; books
and poems everywhere, a catholic
world of reality, roots of Oklahoma
canned in clear jars, waiting
for winter. This cool miracle
weighed heavily, coming from
her slight wallet. But she blessed
this strange room, played cards
with her brother, and called her
friends to spread the word of survival.

TODAY IT MAY RAIN

Today it may rain, but that's no promise
anymore than being an artist means
you're a chipmunk. All night long
the radio issues sorrow as low as the
sound can go. My neighbor, who flings
himself around and throws bricks
on his floor, can sleep through it.
The flowers she bought lasted
so long, all the water disappeared, was
an idea that kept the stalks green. Tulips
bent down in benediction. It all turns
artificial in the gentle way you seek me out.

VERY SMALL SLICES

Buddah is always calm because he puts
a shot of brandy in his black tea.
I am always anxious because I wonder
if the goat chewing on tin in the
parking garage has come to eat
my soup cans. The mixture of truth
and stream of consciousness makes
a strange cake, which I promise to eat
in very small slices. And the church bells,
that rang out so beautifully when I drove
here, distance themselves from me with an
attitude of sameness. How much are we
missing just by having things around us so
unchanged, even the dropping sun becomes
a quick song that the stars forget to memorize.

WARMING

Here in Sacramento's old park
on Alhambra Boulevard, we sit
and talk. The Clunie pool is still
empty. We remember Victoria's
poem about it. The muddy, green
pond floats its ducks and geese.
We sit on a bench beside a man
playing his guitar. This late
winter pleasure floats in our
heads, breaking through memory
as disturbed as the pond's murky
bottom. You tell me a story
about being in another country,
how you and a man chased
a rainbow, stood in it, but it
kept shifting ahead of you. You
couldn't keep the gold of that moment
except now, in remembering.
Far from where we talk, a huge
shelf of ice falls into the ocean
as we watch the ripples
in the water.

A Story And Other Efficiencies

And what kind of cereal did you cheat with /
said the lecturer.

And I told her / Sugar fats.

I knew it / she said.
I knew it.
I knew it.

Sugar-things are *not* allowed.
When are you going to learn
and when will you care enough
to be your very best?

Then the sun came down
striking her on the head
and I said / yeah
it's that old time religion,
fortified with eight
essential deaths,

mine, hers and six others.

Will someone read scripture? / said a victim.

I am a non-believer / said I.

But there is a free baseball card
inside the package / said a victim.

I'm for the 49ers / said I, again /
with numerous nutritive values.

That is not for publication / said someone,

and then a tiger with sugar-frosted tail
came for the get-a-way, and I was ready
for the grrr-rrr-eat escape.

May you drown in nonfat milk / I yelled.
(the tiger, galloping
        galloping)

And may your flakes be eternally limp.

And I rode away.

KATHRYN HOHLWEIN

Kathryn Hohlwein was known as Joyce Jerrell throughout her whole childhood in the Rocky Mountains, at the very foot of our American Mount Olympus in the Wasatch Range.

Though a Unitarian rather than a Mormon, she adored Salt Lake City for its weather, its scenery and its skiing. She studied English and Philosophy and French at the University of Utah and received her Master's In English from Middlebury College at Bread Loaf in the Green Mountains of Vermont.

Thereafter she studied on scholarships in France and Spain, met and married the German artist Hans-Jurgen Hohlwein and they went together to Beirut, both of them to teach there before spending a year in the Highlands of Scotland and then coming to the USA to teach at a series of Universities. They both were Professors at California State University, Sacramento, both with happy careers. They had three children: Reinhard, Andrea and Laura.

After retirement, Kathryn created the Readers of Homer, a non-profit organization that provided all-day or all-night audience participation readings of THE ILIAD and/or THE ODYSSEY of Homer. They have done so many readings they now are known as the International Readers of Homer, and they continue to this day.

Kathryn has loved, studied, taught and written poetry all her life.

My Clarity

In the night, aiming
at a precise accountancy of my living —
as always, the reckoning
overtaken, this time by moonlight
or the slow wavering of the
     camphor tree in it,
in its rippling, echoing chalkiness.

I wanted to keep it unpeopled, simple,
the moonlit grass a dusty black —
to be emerald green in the morning.

But you arrived, and he did,
the children, an aunt I'd forgotten,
her dress and the book she gave me,
a neighbor from Ohio I had never known,
known only her turquoise bathrobe,
her picking up the paper, then
her screen door softly closing.

And these were to stand for self-knowledge?
And these were to be my clarity?

THE LINE OF MY SMALL HORIZON

To pull the line of my small horizon
taut, as if I could grasp that distance.
Then, swollen with what
I take to be achievement,
to let it buckle slightly, creating
the ridges and mountain ranges.
"That is more like reality," I think –
but I know I am not a cartographer,
geographer, surveyor, or even a
good illusionist.

Words and maps just approximate.
The gulley that looks so shallow
took me four days to traverse.

It wasn't even beautiful
though it did have grouse and
staccato lines of quail. It had
scrub oak turning a peachy scarlet
and willows along a faint creek.

Someone could love it there and settle down.
Not me. All I wanted was to hold onto
the sense of my own passing,
the rock shuffle, twig scramble
branch scratching knowledge and scarring –
a small certainty that I was there.

YEATS SAID

Clinging, clinging
to mother's fond conviction
of her daughter's inviolate beauty —
to pool edge, all of the luminous shallows —
an habitual way with the mirror,
to the dear dispositions
of one beloved body.

For out there the water changes.
What drops off is just the beginning.

If we could see from above
we would know how the great shoal
rips are only a turquoise selvedge
of a black and unrippable fabric
whose warp has fifteen dimensions
that weave where no light spins.

Blacker than my black heart
when I cherish my own extinction
is that playground of old dream fears.

Going under is just the beginning.

Achilles is microscopic, weeping on the sand.
Dido, alone again, cries out through
the ghost halls of Carthage
Yeats said even Homer
might be mad as the wind and the snow.

> *Don't do this. Make a list. Think of money.*
> *Don't do this. Make a list. Think of money.*

BLUR

I wonder when memory loses its way

And falters at crossroads and becomes its own blur

And whether we really would want them to stay —

The collisions that hurt us that long brilliant day.

How language seems futile — an unhappy slur

Of all that we wanted and wanted to stay.

I wonder when memory loses its way

And falters at crossroads and becomes its own blur.

Not Present Enough

We are never present enough.
Streetcar, firefly, bed.
What we said and where we said it,
what we thought and did not say.

Nocturne, apricot or kiss,
why we did not feel it deeply,
why we had better things to do.

Tulip, shoulder, smiles,
where our minds were wandering
where good intentions failed.

Twilight, robin, pillow, sage
What we did and where we did it,
what we meant and did not mean,
when we live and how we live it,
when we die and how we die.

Droop

Instead of my mop-like droop
I could droop like white wisteria,
I could think the down pull brightening,
the cascades of weary developing
tumbling softly away.

You'd do better to think of money,
to count it and count it again —

than to mope about wisteria.

THE SHAPE OF JOY

Once knowing that the days would come to end,
they took the shape of joy
and all the patient beauty
that we postponed from day to day
stood shivering and bare.

And there it was:
the glory of the time that we had lost.

    I cup my hands –
a gesture to recapture that sad day.

The seagulls are like fragments of a flag
battering the masts of limping ships.
The stones, a million times renewed,
are burnished with glistening gray.
The sheep, simple and bland, surprised
us in December fog.

    Bronze fern,
soughing of pines and the
filigreed nudeness of trees,
glens where oak leaves still cling
to the gilt and arabesques of fall –
heron and plover and dolphin sometimes
and cormorant, bent in a lean black bow
circling down in his dive – all lovely.

    I cup my hands.
I try to clasp all instants into one –
waiting, waiting, waiting to believe
and saving praises for a later day –
waiting for the beauty that I grieve
because I did not love it in its day.

HEARING THE AMSEL

Hearing the amsel after many years,
its low chanson down the rain-soaked pine,
the German boy whom she would know one day,
know well enough to share three children by,
that soft-voiced artist listening now (in her)
to blackbirds, two of them,
high over Eisenach in the war,
and promising him dreams.

How to describe such intricacies of song,
woven into loopings, crystal sound,
cross-hatched like his lithograph,
stricken – here a patch of darkness,
there of light, and the two together,
once again.
Hearing the amsel that he loved,
the wet notes softer than the rain,
the hard heart faster, sweeps
        across lost decades,
        tries to refigure cause,
        desists and reckons with poems
        that listen in the eyes of children.
        Waking to the amsel that he loved,
        in wettest dawn, under old family quilts,
        and sweating with misunderstandings,
        an American heart remembers
        the sweetest long held largo.

        Hearing again this songbird that he loved –

(this brother, son, this husband, father, man)
she listens to the notes of what sustains.
The amsel brings in too much joy for tears
Singing through shaken leaves across the years.

MY ACTS

Are my acts like the ash I will become
since everything feels ghostly from this striving?
The line-up of these zeroes makes me numb.

They say things make a difference and that some
good thoughts or deeds indeed affect the living —
but my acts are like the ash I will become.

Our caring is refusal to succumb
to our spent error, our inept conniving.
The line-up of these zeroes makes me numb.

And if the evidence that I am dumb
and can impact no hope of hope surviving,
then all my acts are like the dust I will become.

Deep in each night I total up the sum
of what was worth my fragmented surviving.
My acts are like the ash I will become.
The line-up of these zeroes makes me numb.

DAGUERREOTYPE

That Indian couple, cramped
into the narrow telephone booth

look like a daguerreotype
sepia brown from the dust
dimly lit through the
dirty and fogged-up pane.

They cannot move, not much
and stand immobile in
anxious time.

I want it to be good news.
I want nothing bad to have happened.

Their tenderness seems eternal.

A husband and a wife,
Tarascan, very short,
they lean close to each others' breath
as we once thought
true lovers forever would —
her head upon his chest,
her thorough comfort.

Iwant it to be good news.
I want nothing bad to have happened.

Of course I must take a picture.
How else do we remember?

ON FIGHTING IN BEAUTIFUL PLACES

We share this rage like sex.
It binds me at the heel.
It comes to us like lust,
clamoring when the sky is soft.
Lights glimmer on the river
we came this far to see.

There are times when I can look
death in the face
and say yes yes
I know I know
but those times are rare
and when they occur
I'm convinced I've
already gone mad.

It is severe. The ankles know it...
yes. The throbbing just above
behind the arm pits knows it, too.

Small boys in white pressed shorts
might come to us and smile or
we might wave to them in quiet.
Give them a little something.

But in the distance yellow curs roam
and recede in the ochre dust.

Then I enter our promises —
a familiar country
bristling with insurrection.

My eyes are bandaged
and you know it.
You lead me like a hostage
toward some justice.

Beyond the bandages I hear
the local band strike up. I might
have guessed that lanterns lit
bob red on the festive stream.

The rage coils around
within me, pleads reprieve.

I have been told that I am beautiful
by men who live in worlds
very different from yours,
who know the ancient olive trees
they sit beneath, leaning at
tilted tables, will bear black
fruit a thousand years or more.

But no reprieve, no squad, no fire.
Only the river darkening,
the trial ended, the jury hung.

THE PLEASURE OF RUINS

In a grinding burst the grain
the Peter Iresdale was carrying
exploded out like any wasted seed
into an encircling ocean.

Hull, cabin, men, each bolt,
the Captain's log no doubt,
the double mast wrecked off Olympia
unlucky, and far from Santa Anna.
Intentions of trade and prosperity
grounded to some strange beauty,
such as we might call modern art.

Placed. It seems, along the gleam of coast,
lifted like its glistening cargo
to a subtle and nuanced series
of sundered, luminous metal
that seemed to make of chaos
the ideal, quiet statement.

Of what? "Quiet statement" of what?
Of profit, of expectation,
of strangling and going down?

Still, it could not have been better —
sunk so tight no surf can get it —
each angle of shorn freighter
a clean and original sculpture
sheering the changing light —
a random plot, ugly , amuck,
and we stand there, admiring.
We find its wildness soothing.
We talk as at a museum,
moving in sacrosanct hush,
as if this little stretch of shore
had been awarded a Guggenheim
to play around with the "Peter Iresdale".
We marvel at form and eloquence
of blasted iron strung across the sand.

What future beauty in today's collisions?
The wholly horrid rusting random —
satisfying, scary, and deeply struck.

AFTER SEEING "A THIN RED LINE"

It's not very different from Homer –
the light-disembodied canopy,
the halting advance in fog.
Here this face is stricken.
Here this body twitches
with fear first, death next.
The men sit in mud, like sculpted knots
without expression, eyes - glistening –
the dirtied hands held tight.
The music doesn't swell, but silence does.
Grass divides as creatures pass
and then some others, with a click.

I have a student, experienced but shy
who shows me the small print leather-
bound copy of the Iliad, which
belonged to her mother's father –
before he took his own life.

"I didn't know my grandfather, but
now I'm reading this poem along
with him. Traceries in light pencil,
a few tender asterisks, or
shadowy tentative brackets –
our only conversation."

When Helen can't find her brothers
and worries where they are —
(perhaps they are ashamed of
the slut who is their sister.....)
she looks down from the high wall of
Ilium, past her husband and former Greek friends
and determines she cannot find them
amid the obscuring dirt.

Then Homer tells us so simply
that they are already dead,
 "far away in the land of their fathers,
with the life-giving earth upon them."

"Look at this!" said my student.
"My grandfather marked this passage.
There are two small pencil marks here.
It's like finding him for the first time —
finding him in the dark."

BLEAK INTERVALS

I am gnawing at the mightily worked —
over bone of my extinction.
I yap at it.
It lies there white and dry.
I try to stare it down. It goes on
lying dormant, dull and tasting
no more of something spirited
or real, delivering.

This labor wears me out.
Here it arrives again,
the trippy sun, the ever-
returning envelope, sealed and
again resealed.

I hear the black fact rush me,
locomotive in falling snow —
its alien yellow light.
Sweet Keats, I ache for you,
wishing on your star.
your bones extinguishing coughs.

I press upon the still
full sockets of my skull till
harried little dots emboss
the expansive blackness.
They pepper the thick terrain of
endless inward me, alive.

Of course
I think of Yorick. He, at least
had made the company laugh, —
laughter cascading down the fog
between bleak intervals of drink
in Denmark's wintery light.

And I think of
how delicate the creatures are,
considerate, abandoning no bones
for us to trip upon, or shatter
with our spades. How well they
hide from us
(who are afraid)
the nuisance of their deaths.

They don't care to remind us of Auschwitz,
or give signals of our mayhem
(except when they cross the streets),
of cannibals in our streets and hatreds
intered in our muscles.

Ah, Poetry.

You made me think like this.

A stern acquaintance brought these
thoughts to term – acceptance of Rwanda,
the terrible dragging of Hector,
all genocides forever

and my friendly mother dead.

POEM WITHOUT IMAGES

I no longer want the absolute truth.
If I had it, it might incline me to
pass judgment on how you wash your feet
or how you prepare for sleep.
And, once I dislike how you sleep,
I will surely despise how you dream,
especially if you twitch in the dreaming,
especially if you value your dream.

Your dream is defined now heretical,
and my truth requires it be stomped.
I will not tolerate these images,
dark in your night time soul.

So, in fairness, I put your dream on trial
and I can because I am rich.
The trial is rigged by my truth,
which insists it is objective,
but likes me much better than you,
by God!

Your dream is apparently illegal,
ill-got and ill-conceived and, after
due consideration, it's out —
your bath, your feet, your sleep,
your twitch, your dream, your
once-in-a-lifetime you.

DEAR POEM

Dear Poem, I thank you
for your insouciance,
your weird unnerving aptitude
to say the unprepared for.
You're the best thing in my life
and though I walk right past you,
and though I vacuum past you,
you have my real respect.

I know you don't believe this,
scattered as you are in notebooks,
abandoned among the bills.
But you're what I think of when dreaming.
You stand there without expression,
patient and never the same.
You're indifferent if I feel trespassed
and endure me if I am scared.

You are like the tree, the giant elm
equivalent to my skyline
that I needed back then as a child
to lean my forehead against
calmed by its cellular truth.

CHÈRE MAÎTRE

Among the other things I learned
this year that Flaubert, cranky and
isolate (after his mama died)
wrote tenderly to Georges Sand
who had given up cigars
for the making of pinafores.
Bohemian life had receded,
seemed odd. All those trousers,
swagger, all those words,and men.

She fingered her inherited brooch
and wrote
"Chère maître" — weird usage of the
feminine, as though Flaubert were her
sister. *"Chère maître — You are too
hard on life. Go take a walk
and note the tiny blossoms. Then
you will feel better."*

He didn't — do either,
but wrote for her, for *her!*
"A Simple Heart ," the story of
one named Felicité, — old, poor, stooped
and stupid, who radiated love, for whom
love was
not only enough (strange thought!),
for whom it was not yet a word,
not a virtue, not an attribute,
but was what made all circulate,
breathe, what air does,
a direction of the heart.

IN JANUARY

In January the Janissarie asked the functionary at the sanctuary of the cemetery if it was customary and necessary or compulsory to write an obituary for the mortuary.

He said it was.

In February the Fiduciary (who was a local luminary) for the regulatory of the bestiary and the aviary of the migratory went epistolary, even literary, and wrote an at first explanatory, complimentary, conciliatory and exploratory note but then found the vocabulary of an adversary and signed an accusatory, recriminatory, admonitory letter to the judiciary of the repository at the library on the promontory. He knew in his pituitary that it was mostly monetary, but hoped it might be temporary. Or maybe just subsidiary and secondary.

But he was angry. VERY!

March was less harsh.

To St. Thomas Aquinas

*~ How many angels, really, can dance on
the head of a pin? ~*

The answer to the question of how many
angels can dance on the head of a pin
is seven hundred and thirty one.

On the outer rim five hundred angels
line dance the hora or miserlou
with their wings packed each to the other
like monarchs who've flown from Canada
to nestle tightly in Mexico.

They never stop. They never stop.
Nor do those in the next big circle
composed of two hundred angels.
They move in the other direction
and have more space between them.

Then there's the circle of thirty
who dance like Isadora,
their wings and footsteps close
and they dance with great abandon.
In the center is the prima ballerina
pirouetting ecstatically.

She can spread her transparent wings
over the whole ensemble.

Sometimes
I think she is waving to me, but
it's just a formal position.

A pious rabbi in Padua
once thought there were 231,
but he is to be forgiven.
It was only the fourteenth century
and he was always needing new lenses.
He could not see the turning whirr
of the angels dancing the rim.
He thought it was just the shape
of the pin, gleaming and glinting in sparkles.

But now we have fiber optics
and can witness the tiniest ankle
and the slightest blur of white light
encircling them all.

THE CITY OF POMEGRANATE

The city of pomegranate
is way ahead of us
in terms of city planning.
Even the outskirts are welcoming.
Thick, waxy bright orange blossoms
designate direction, and star like
begin constellations that become
geodesic domes, heavily
rounded red balls.

Inside, communal as opened sunflowers.
astonishing city planning,
each unit comfy and safe.
A translucent membrane
instead of a fence, more
like a Japanese screen
divides the spaces between them.

The red light districts are uniform,
so that is taken care of.
There is no grid, just winding
streets and rosy cul-de-sacs,
with equal light shining
on them and from them.

Only a few are bedridden,
marginal, pale, and stuck –
but still they love their own homes.
Most are briskly vigorous and
look like they just took a shower –
each one a single jewel
ready to pop out and serve.

Around each bend is a gospel
choir that sings "Hallelujah !

Amen."
And look at all that radiance!

In My Driveway

I wonder if I could convince you
that a snail's tracks made me think
of Bach's Well-Tempered Clavichord.

Would you believe me when I assert
that they weren't there last night but
completely there this morning?
That its little smear steps were
stitched across the driveway
as if a consummate seamstress
had put them precisely there,
so good she could sew on concrete?

Their steady even purpose
left a trail of clarity,
even of meaningfulness
in the pearly translucent intention.
Tiny, perfect rectangles
seemed like pure lucidity.
Bach is gone, the snail is gone
and we never spoke or met.

But I marvel at the application
of miniature perfections,
one after the other, the other.,
evenly spaced like beads on a string,
particulates in a wave.

I don't know where they would take
us, these undulating patterns —
but I am sure they're not forlorn
nor do they seem like nowhere.
They go where I can't follow —
precise inscribed notations .

Oh! Rosaries of Joy!
underneath the engine —
and each one has a certitude,
a certitude like faith.

WHAT MY GRANDDAUGHTERS SEE

Two of my granddaughters
like to watch me sleep
at least they think I am asleep, and
I wonder what they see.
White hair on white pillow,
wrinkled arms caught in sheets.
My little snort delights them
and they giggle and shush each other
thinking I do not know
how much fun they are having.

I do not mind at all though
it is strange to be stared at.
I just wonder what they see:
The spooky dark flow of my longings,
the poem-giver inside me?

ARCHING IN MOONLIGHT

Proclus has assured me
the heliotrope has its special
prayer, that precisely prayer
is its doing as it follows the sun's
course through the day.

The selenotrope, its cousin, likewise
prays its best as in moonlight
it silently arches, loving that
silvery light.

Could we hear
their rotations, the air
softly buffeted,
petals would sing hymns
to their king, such as is
within their powers.

IN THE ROANJIN GARDEN

In the Roanjin Garden, I sat for hours.
Everyone sits there for hours.
Rocks and sand, gravel and rocks,
stones and mottled wall,
white gravel, raked, and dark large stones.
Oneself still saying whatwhat
oneself asking, looking round, asking.

Having met, loved, married and died with
Masashi Hara, I could still hear him repeating.

"Shibui."

If whale or Buddha, turtle or settled bird —
this mind and that mind begin to move
through the white curled spaces between.
Will it surface and spout, stretch and retrace —
settle feather by feather in stillness?

Even at twenty-five, you, my lost real husband —
would have settled into that stone
would have floated in that curve of gravel
while I was busy quoting.
You were a quiet young artist
but later, agitation —
flapping and cawing flapping, flapping
and this was all you were wanting,
though you called it
"The Art of the Fugue."

From where we sit we can count
fourteen stones and the fifteenth
is always missing.
Like those four tailing notes
of Bach's final work
resolution remains beyond us.

I sit here, remembering your listening –
Bach's name in notes =

B   A   C   H

Mysterious as the Buddha
that concludes as this floating sea does.
And I look for you as I knew you.
You died this very day –
white petal, Shibui wall.

You entered the fugue and became it
You see the fifteenth stone.

ON BACH'S "AIR" FROM SUITE # 3

This truth is strange we are not what we are
Most of the time we barely even care
If we rise slightly, silent as a star.

That weekend you were tinkering with the car
I turned and saw your face shine and your hair.
This truth is strange we are not what we are.

We merchandize our poisons, eat at tar.
Despite our weak, our scared, our stuttering prayer
We can rise lightly, silent as a star.

We think we cannot love except from far
Across the sterile distances we share.
This truth is strange we are not what we are.

Fear is the tearing greed that begets war.
We kill our gracious world yet anywhere
We still rise quietly, silent as a star.

Clarity becomes us even in the dark
And sends a comfort through the holy air.
This truth is strange we are not what we are
But do rise brightly, silent as a star.

WALT WHITMAN IS STILL
IN LOVE WITH ME

Walt Whitman is still in love with me,
and I return his love.
But he loves you too, and your children
and even their children beyond.
He thinks we all are beautiful,
he loves to hear us speak.
He says we have beautiful voices —
a soft poetic speech.
He knows that inside we are artists,
American, and deep.
Physically we are splendid,
outlined against the water.
We are kind to our lost baby brothers
and consider the harlot our friend.

How he does this is way beyond me,
but I try to believe in him.

I want to make him happy.

KATHRYN HOHLWEIN

DOES GOD EVER GET TIRED OF
"MOVING IN MYSTERIOUS WAYS"?

I think he does not.
He does get bored by our conviction
of his mysterious ways, and finds us transparent and dull.

He thinks we make up mysteries
and assign them to his caprice, but observes
that our many connivings, our unscrupulous manifold
intrigues just create clever conditions
for what we then call mysteries.

On the other hand, he does feel dazzled and dizzied
by real mysteries beyond his control. The warp and weft
of magnetic waves, the weird threads holding the scenery,
the breadth of the multiverse.

Sometimes he looks down upon us
and finds us sort of darling,
but that is about the whole story.
Of course, that is just what we long for.

ORCHARD XVI

Almost lost in circumference
I need to rejoin the world.
I gravitate outwards towards
the blinding stripe of mustard,
a sizzling yellow edge
that starts where the orchard ends.
It is a surrounding brilliance
that plays havoc with location.
It is red-winged blackbird heaven
but it makes my life feel dizzy.
Concentric thinking wants me
and I love the shield, the circle.
Still, in brightness I lurch out
to the riddle of linear time,
to the sixty year-old child,
the seven-year-old crone.
Women's voices drift like pollen.
They call back and forth like starlings,
glossy and flushed out of hiding.
I embrace myself like a basket
piled high with available blessings.

POLE-VAULTING TO NIRVANA

Hop-scotching towards Nirvana,
the easy knees reassuring, the
rubber-heel-toss lots of fun.
But here a choice is exploding.
There a decision glimmering.
Still, play is a form of gratitude
and delight a kind of prayer.
Twilight is always a comfort,
the valley lights coming on.
And mother plays the piano.
But the path itself obscured
by blossoms, thistles, and berries.

Leap-frogging towards Nirvana,
using the back of Brahms,
lifting from the strength of Homer.
An influence in the doorway –
one of the beautiful teachers
one of the beautiful guides.
And now my taste being formed,
identical to my being.
And I still loving the gloaming,
still adoring Bach.
The lovely children leaving
and the students growing older.
The astonishing kiss a signpost.
The bed of loving a gift.
And the path itself less hidden
Though fog and sandstorms cloud it.

Pole-vaulting to Nirvana,
with pacemaker and cane.
A certain joy in forgiveness,
a pleasure in recollection.
my brunette frame now a photo,
the dance movement cancelled out.
Students nearing retirement,
and grandchildren testing their names.
The world itself a confusion —
both bitter and radiant.
And the path itself lit softly
with the glow of splendid friendships,
and the luminous music of Mozart.
I rock, I rock to get ready
and my eyes are fixed on the height.
I propel myself down the well-worn path.
I plant my cane in the tight little box ,
take off — to maybe twenty feet,
then clear the bar forever.

VICTORIA DALKEY

Victoria Dalkey is the long time art critic for the Sacramento Bee. She is the author of two chapbooks *twenty.nine poems* and *In the Absence of Silver* and co-author with Kay Lyndsey of a third, *Map of the Pearl*. With composer and guitarist Gilda Taffett, she collaborated on *sub rosa*, a composition for guitar, soprano, and spoken word. She received a B.A. in English and an M.A. in Poetry Writing from California State University, Sacramento, where she studied with Clyde Enroth, Dennis Schmitz, Kathryn Hohlwein, and Olivia Castellano. She is a past participant in the Squaw Vallery Writer's Conference Poetry Program. With her husband artist Fred Dalkey, she participated in *In Lak'Ech: A Collaboration of Vision and Voice* at the Southern Pacific Depot warehouse, which received a grant from the Sacramento Metropolitan Arts Commission.

ON READING ARACELIS GIRMAY'S THE BLACK MARIA

A storm is on the way.
Acacias rain golden flowers
under a darkening sky.

Aracelis tells us a tale of black grief
fattened in a slave ship's hold.
A storm is on the way.

Black lives matter, we shout today
marching for Trayvon or Freddie Gray
under a darkening sky.

A cowbird king and his greedy offspring
connive with thieves in towering bowers.
A storm is on the way.

They dine with the Chinese head of state
at the luxurious club at Mar-a-Lago
under a darkening sky.

Missiles rain bombs on a Syrian night
while children fight for breath.
Another storm has come today
under a pitch black sky.

CROWS
for Tom Philippe

Outside dissident crows flap
tarry wings, puff up oiled
feathers then settle down, sleek
projections complicating the geometry of trees.

One struts, head jutting as he paces,
marshaling strays, calling out crude orders.
A few shoot out from branches and back,
black yo-yos on invisible strings.

Inside, the high window in the dining room
becomes a mirror, a blinding band of light
you can't look into or at. Something
is moving but I can't see it. Blinded

by sun, limbs stiff with inertia, I hear
it moving, under the light westward
with the crows. The phone rings.
A young woman, crying, tells me

a painter whose last show I didn't see
is dead, killed on the road near Point Arena.
Can I write about it, she asks, explain
the importance of his life and death?

I say I'll do what I can, knowing
I can't do anything, can't revise
his life or transform his death, can't
give him his last review, can't

find any words to help her, can't
even find the meaning of the crows
in this poem I keep writing in the dark.

MARY THEOBALD: WINTER OF '52

She was 17 when snow began to fall.
It fell until the lake was whited out, the town
cut off, the highway over Donner Pass
shut down, S.P. freight trains stalled
in ramshackle sheds at Norden.

The storm went on for days
trainmen trapped, food scarce,
toilets full, Mary and her folks
hungrier by the day. She dreamed
of summer when she would leave
for college at U.O.P. – faux ivy league
school in flat farmland where tomatoes,
asparagus, pears, and walnuts grew.

At least they had wood for fire
could melt snow to drink.
They didn't know the brakemen
in the snowed-over tunnels
were hungry too. One, called
Wild Bill when he drank, lost
his paycheck at the casino,
pawned his father's watch in Reno,
kept their spirits up with corny jokes.

At last planes came, dropped
food as if on war torn camps
in Korea. Mary and Bill survived.
but never met. The snow melt came,
houses at Tahoe shed white coats,
the trains began to run again.

28 years after the storm, Bill, 76,
died at Mercy Hospital in the valley
kidneys failed, all systems shut down.
At 80, Mary, died in the valley too
during a thunder storm, the heavens
opening up to welcome her.

PORTRAIT OF MY HUSBAND AS AN ITALIAN PLUM

The tree practices
its multiplication tables.

Morning blossom
times

evening blossom
equals

the black dog
who follows wherever you go.

Petals drop
on the darkening lawn.

The fireflies of our cigarette tips
circle

until the tree disappears
like one heart

into another. Soon
we'll lose track of the days

forget again to pick
the small, tart crop.

Though one low-hanging
plum, saved from birds,

will remain, ripe
enough to sweeten a tongue.

THE YARD LONG BEANS

The yard long beans
wound themselves around
taut strings to the top
of the green stick frame
we built to tame them
and rioted for two months
purple blossoms out each morning
tiny shoots set under the moon each night.

Hungry for green
we picked them each day
too soon sometimes
tender and boneless as baby fingers
so Emile at five complained and wouldn't
eat them
so soon snatched tangled from the vine
and fried with pork and garlic.

We ate till sated with green
and still they came
writhing in on themselves
pencil-slim dark arm-long beans
dangling from the harp-strung strings.

August over we forgot them
passed them for late tomatoes
red at last, fat as breasts
and warm in our hands
and for seductive eggplant
midnight skinned, white fleshed
and sliced for frying
fragrant as green apples.

Even Emile forgot
to go out in the evening
and braid the vines
in and out the strings
and urge the beans on.

But tonight he remembered.
I heard him call
and I went out to the frame
collapsed on itself
the boy holding up
a stringer of beans
that had grown too far
inside the vine to reach.

They were yellow and knotted
as an old cigar smoker's fingers
and long as the boy's legs.
The fallen vine rattled
in the wind as Emile
brushed an ant from his arm
and said *I'm sorry Mother.*

BONKEI: A MODEL OF THE DELTA
for Wayne

I look through the bungalow window
see you again, an ordinary man
working, bent over the table,
on a model of the Delta:
green felt fields, furrows
of dried clay, mazy mirror-
shard rivers that come to a point
at the whipped paper sea.

You place a tiny, Chinese farmer
near a row of scallions snipped
from dark green plastic; light
overhead casts deep red
shadows on the world you make.

Cold, I stand on the porch, teeth
chattering against the glass.
You come out and lay
a work-warm finger
on my blue lips.

CHINOISERIE

The woman at the gallery wears
a necklace of kingfisher feathers
bluer than the lips of ten thousand
blue-bodied dancers.

She tells me no birdsong
fills the still air of China now.
Only the homely laughter of ducks
dropping eggs in red dust
breaks the quiet of the countryside.

Wild birds were a threat to the grain
she says, pointing to the necklace
with a hand whose veins are bluer
than the insides of certain flowers
once gathered on Kun Lun Mountain.

WELL-KNOWN TEA

Searching for tea at Ho Chin market
my husband found an unfamiliar packet
marked *Well-Known Tea*.

It must be famous, he said. Knowing
how tricky translation can be, I ventured,
It might mean 'common tea' or 'everyday tea'.

The first taste told us the tea lacked
character, didn't have the good dirt
taste of Pu-erh, earthy as beets,

or the pungent smell of Lapsang Souchong
filling our nostrils with memories of chill
autumn air and burning leaf-piles.

It lacked the clarity of pale green
Iron Goddess of Mercy,
soother of raw nerves.

Centuries ago in Yunnan Province
golden buds and soft green leaves
were plucked by virgins fed on food

devoid of flavors that might linger
tainting the delicate taste
of a liquid meant to be sipped

while contemplating Okakura Kakuzo's
beautiful foolishness of things.
We thought of how things were

and how they are and sipped
the *Well-Known Tea*
which turned out to be

good enough after all.

LISTENING TO BACH'S DOUBLE
CONCERTO IN D MINOR

You understand why he had so many children.
The big chords of the opening
fat and dark
heavy as your husband's balls
in your hand
making love in summer
all the weight of his being
concentrated in the soft,
loaded, lightly furred, moist
heat of the testes.

Does the small boy know
as he practices his scales
testicles tucked up tight to his body
the joy he will feel one day
as he plays
after the *vivace*
the *largo?*

Does he sense in his tentative scrapings
how the bow will fall on the strings
largo, ma non tanto, non tanto,
exciting them as the lining
of a woman's uterus is excited
by the sight of her lover?

In the coming together
the moving forth
the call and response of the strings
they are gathered together –
the father of twenty children
the small boy practicing his scales
the woman who is both mother and lover –
in the pure, sexual music of praise.

LOOKING INTO ALBINUS' ANATOMY

I

Who is this rawboned
rattleboned, slimsy fellow

strolling through the picnic grounds
bare boned, bag of bones

striking an elegant pose
rackabones, rattlebones

phalanges clicking
backbone ticking

gray and grinning, gangle
shanks, giggle bones

worn to a shadow
worn to the bones?

II

Imagine your skeleton in a northern light
in a freezing cold barn in the lowlands
laid out on a table heaped with snow
then strung up from the ceiling with ropes
and pulleys to look like a traveler
in a melancholy landscape

the pale inevitable
wandering in a pastoral setting
pausing by a stone mausoleum,
a huge tomb set down among trees,

pining for a woman in a red skirt
peasant blouse tied up under
her breasts, brown waist bared,
skin soft, girdle of muscle
supple around the rib cage
vertebrae dimpled down the spine
like a line of pearls.

BECHE DE MER

They parade a giant phallus
down Capitol Avenue
pulled by tiny men
festive in short sleeved shirts
and summer pants. Its magnificent head
breaks through the arcade of trees
brushing against leaves, dusty and thick,
that shut out the burning sun.

Enormous, erect, pink prick,
what do you mean to me?
Why do you enter my dream
just moments ago serene
as a photographer's gray card?

I have seen you before
attached to a crude
small figure of Pan
in a Picasso drawing
and in Japanese prints
monstrous and wrinkled
slouching like a giant sea slug –
beche de mer –
toward your target, inching
hairily toward ecstasy.

In this dream you are detached
even cerebral, lofting your way
down the avenue, an object of amazement
and worship. I imagine you flying up
poised over Tower Bridge
pointing out over the river
toward the shining granaries
and burnt rice fields,
shimmering in the sun
with salt and semen.

ODD FELLOWS LAWN

At Odd Fellows Lawn in the old city cemetery
I sip tea with Julia, my wished for sister
and opposite – the small quick, angular woman
who darts around my sluggish body,
stabbing me with chilled salad forks
nights I can't sleep – and sits here
materialized in front of me, pouring
Lapsang Souchong into a thin bone cup.

She has invited me here because she wants me
to learn a lesson about tradition, about how
the dead comfort us with their propriety.
I have come because she has chosen
for her classroom the graveyard
I lived next door to as a child, listening
every night to the giant machine of the dead
pulsing in the earth as I fought off sleep,
the graveyard I passed every morning, crossing
carefully to the other side of the street, sometimes
walking blocks out of my way so as not to see
the tall stones and mausolea rising
out of the trees on my way to school.
This is the lesson I was always late for.

Like the child striving for invisibility
in the classroom where her answers are always wrong
I am a phantom, sitting here, smelling rank flowers
and sweet, listening to the whirr of small birds
in the trees, dipping a thin cookie in tea
until, like me, it dissolves, dulling
the brimming liquid in the cup.
The blue and white cloth spread in front of us

the English picnic basket and silver thermos
are not real either. They are thought forms
like Julia's transparent hand, passing me
a cucumber sandwich, her voice suddenly my mother's
as she dragged me down the dark street, repeating,
It's not the dead you have to fear, but the living.

Once I saw myself clearly in my coffin
the too white skin made bright with embalmer's rouge
and once I imagined peeling the dead pelt down
stepping out clean, glad to be rid of that coat.
I smoke too many cigarettes because I want to die
sooner than later (though not too soon)
but I have never been a ghost before
sitting lightly on the corpse of the earth
rising up and walking toward myself through the trees.
I listen for the clink of bones beneath my feet
the sound of bodies slopping down into slime
the hearts of the dead beating sleep into the earth
but hear only the small talk of birds
and the tap-tap of Julia's light feet
behind me, falling rhythmically on rich soil.

CHARMIN' BILLY

I don't know where to put the beat-up table
I can't part with because my father painted it.

Can't find the right place for this half-moon
with three squat legs joined by pegs

something out of a tale about a girl
held prisoner by a dwarf, forced to spin

straw into gold, or the one about the princess
locked in a tower until she let her hair down.

Daddy was handsome as a prince that day whistling
Can she bake a cherry pie, Billy Boy, Billy Boy?

as he covered the table with a green
dark as the deepest pines in the forest

long before I guessed his real name.

On The Seacoast Of Bohemia

Wasn't there a trained bear
wandering through the scene
escapee from a family circus
a mother who rode bareback
father who bent steel
boy who swallowed fire?

The painter adopted a child's style
but couldn't hide the cruelty:
bear muzzled, prodded to ride a scooter,
ringmaster father snapping the whip
boy in clown paint hanging on a horse's tail
the woman circling
endlessly, endlessly.

DRAGONFLY SUMMER

Over the pond, hovering,
the small ones we called darning needles
weave in and out long grass,

the large ones, hung in air,
fixed then darting
with a quick blue blur

a thunderous buzz
near the ear. A nymph
red as terra cotta,

sits in a Double Bubble pink
plastic wading pool
frozen in fear.

She does not hear
the dragonfly young
called nymphs too

stalking their prey, shooting
their long underlips or masks
to catch larvae or tadpoles.

Eye-minded already
they target only the moving
leaving the fixed alone

as the girl in the pool
who stares into empty blue sky
framed in the eye of a dragonfly.

EASTER SUNDAY

Snapshot by the pond: slant light falling jagged
on the new green world. Mother in pink suit
with padded shoulders, brother in blue serge
and me, awkward would-be ballerina in yellow ruffles
white shoes white gloves. No father, of course.
Was he there, taking the picture? Not likely.
The pond's in the picture, deep and dark
the fountain spray glinting in the sunlight.
The old frog, hidden in the rocks, watches
the pregnant carp, white skin sloughing off gold.
Later, I'll dive in, let the fish bite my thighs
cleanse myself of church, father, redemption
the risen Christ floating up over the pond
as I wash myself in the dark waters.

BLUE SKIES

Fallen on the sodden grass
wings spread, legs pulled up in prayer
even the dead dragonfly
lures the eye. In your hand it lights

fixed in terminal flight,
slender wings lined with gold,
the green thorax, swollen hard
camellia bud above the trunk —

a bundle of long muscles
for the quick beat of long wings —
the great jeweled eyes wrapped
around the head so you can see

in the mesh of lenses one thousand pictures
of the last thing seen.
The long tail, shot with blue —
turquoise, faience — reminds you

the most beautiful things you see
are a function of imperfection
an interference of light
falling on mother of pearl

or kingfisher feathers. Not color
but the absence of color
confusing the eye into seeing
translucent blue skies.

BONNARD

painted winsome women over and over
playing croquet at dusk in a checkerboard dress,
at the gray-green end of day,
or dining alone with an insistent pet cat
who reaches a paw for the fish on her plate.

Later one bathes in capacious claw-foot tubs
dissolving in water, blue, green, violet,
flesh fleeing in an aqueous shimmer,
long-legged Marthe, his wife, neurasthenic
turned inward, oblivious of his gaze.

Some say he was full of sorrow, dejected.
He wrote: *He who sings is not always happy.*
But he filled the air with luminous yellows
with mauve and purple and electric blue
and the redolent scent of ripening fruit.

POMEGRANATE SEEDS
for F.D.D.

Burst open on the tree
this pomegranate
tells me to crush its seeds
make ink and write scarlet songs.

*   *   *

In Spain the Sisters strain
the juices humming Scarlatti.

*   *   *

Once I stole a pomegranate
on the way to school
and bit the strange protruding fruit.
The juice stained my white skirt.
Bittersweet curse.

*   *   *

Persephone only ate three seeds
for which she paid dearly.

*   *   *

I love to watch you eating pomegranates.
Split open with your small sharp knife
the seeds wait for your mouth to fall on them
greedy as a bear with a honeycomb.

*   *   *

No temperate Greek, Eve
filled her mouth with seeds
and spit them in a stream
into Adam's open mouth.

   *   *   *

Once you brought me a whole bowlful
of pomegranate seeds heaped up
and spooned some into my mouth
before you buried your face in the bowl.

   *   *   *

Consider the Rose Window of Chartres
if you think the pomegranate an unholy fruit.

   *   *   *

One hot September day
you laid me down in the shade
of the pomegranate tree
and smeared my temples
with the juices of the fruit.

   *   *   *

Thus did Solomon soothe
Sheba in her waning years.

READING A USED BOOK
with apologies to John Crowe Ransom

I savor the smear
of a chocolate thumbprint
on the last stanza of a song
in which two spectral lovers
touch fingers that flutter
like a bird whose song
shall never be heard

linger over the splatter
of spaghetti sauce on the page
where, full of long white arms
and milky skin, a man remembers
a thousand sins

run my finger over the round,
raised, thickened spot
where a drop, tear or spittle,
fell on the noon-apple dreams
of the scuttling geese
John Whiteside's daughter chased.

How I long to touch this lover
of dark chocolate, Italian food
and tart, succulent words.
I follow his spoor,
keen as the leaping borzoi
on the book's blue cover,
sniffing for traces of musk
along white streams meandering
through the dark forest of barbed marks
but only the thick, yellow
odor of old books lingers.

It is late. The sheets are cold.
Dog-eared, I slip myself
under the covers. Toes curled
I dream of pears – sinuous Boscs
in plain brown wrappers – and you
in your kitchen years from now,
reading this poem in a used book.

INTERSECTION: 34TH AND R

It is a crossing of crosses, a set of all sets:
Latin Cross, Tau Cross, Greek Cross,
Papal Cross, Cross of Lorraine.
It is a crosswalk we come to at cross purposes.

You are looking for the pale beauty you glimpsed
yesterday by the three stone pines that rise
dark and elegiac behind the cyclone fence
the elusive one who holds the key to your secret life
the changeless one who changes minute by minute.
I, on the other hand, am looking for Mrs. Beevis
the jowly, wheezing, snub-nosed, flat-faced woman
who lived next door to us on C Street in the 1950s.

I search for her ghost, stumping along on doughy legs
knotted with blue varicosities, white scarf flapping
toward Libby's in a milky dawn rinsed with tomato juice,
pressed blood of the love fruit condensed in white smoke
rising over the tracks where scarlet globes climb
conveyor belts to the mouth of the ivy covered cannery
where she worked the early shift every summer.

We wait, pale and dissatisfied, in the predawn light
looking down the nave of this strange church, whose apse
stretches from the power poles of the SMUD substation
to the Romanesque facade of the now bare-brick cannery.
A small man in a red cap, smug with morning prayers,
jogs past the arcade of sad arches on the facade
of the old Hollywood Furniture Store (now Yokohama Tires).

Dawn breaks over the substation, lighting up
its orange towers – dancing angels of electricity –
burning us into a grudging love. Our lady has come –
yours and mine. She is one, she is the same,
doughy-legged, white-scarved, lovely as the dawn.

Letter To Q

I met a famous artist the other day
at the bronze foundry. You know his work,
full of *duende* like yours, his figures always
going into the dark or coming out of it.

He grabbed my hand and said:
My son put the clay in my hands.
I couldn't do anything after my wife died.
Sixty years we were together.
Every day we talked.
I don't think she understood my work
but she had good instincts.
Now my son hands me the clay
to model the heads for the bronze.
I work all day making these masks.
But the nights are bad and the weekends.

He held on to me as if afraid I wouldn't stay.
We sat, held hands, watched his son pick up
a blow torch, melt the bronze skin
with a roaring blue flame, the patina blooming
on a skull-like head, a pitted face with a long
nose and empty eyes. He said it was a mask
like the ones they wear in Iraq
in the Green Zone, where it's safe.
I think of him now, how he wasn't
in the Green Zone that day,
how he never got back.

DIGGING IN EL SALVADOR: EL MOZOTE

Gently they brush the dirt away
from delicate ribcages, finger bones
curled like ferns, a doll sized pelvis.
Around the font where the children were baptized,
the last thing left of the church that welcomed their births,
they pile up skulls, tagged with red stickers
to show where the bullets entered.

The truth comes out bone by bone
all smaller than the bones of Lucy
buried in the African earth long ago
unearthed and rearranged into human form for the camera
small bones stitched together like a sampler.
We are all one, her bones said. We are in this together.

The truth comes out bone by bone
jumbled in the rubble of the church
where the older children learned to sing and sew
to say their catechisms and Our Fathers
where the youngest, who new only *milk* and *mother*
learned *gun* and *soldier* on their last day.

The truth comes out, a red sticker for each lie
the lies we were told, the lies we told ourselves
and this time the bones tell us: We are not one.
We are many and this is what we do to each other.
As for Lucy, she died a long time ago.

HIS FAVORITE

All morning, Ina, I have been thinking of you
hoping you are wandering in Paradise
whatever Paradise is for you. I keep wanting
to place you in a Persian miniature
cool as sherbet in a mint green gown
walking in a landscape of palace gardens lined with gold,
in gardens evenly dotted with small explosions
of wild flowers and leaping gazelles.

I hope you are there with a prince who loves you
under a crescent moon hung in a dark blue sky
scattered with stars even in daytime.
I hope your body has been restored
that your bruises and cuts are healed
that your skull, blasted away, has reformed.

In truth, Ina, I don't know what Paradise
would be for you. Perhaps a bowl of hot soup
and a piece of bread eaten in peace with your family
and then an uneventful stroll through the park.
Maybe a trip to Euro-Disney or a day in Dubrovnic
before the war began. Whatever it is, I wish it for you.

But I know that your body still lies hidden
deep in the Bosnian forest, your body and the bodies
of your sisters. Indicted for war crimes in Sarajevo,
he recites their names: Amela, Enisa, Alma, and Misa
Mejra and Sehra. But you, Ina, you were his favorite,
he says, the man who raped you, marched you
into the woods and shot you in the back of the head.

He didn't enjoy it, he says, raping you and your sisters
raping you with his brothers in a gang, taking turns
until they were all done. He didn't enjoy it
yet you were his favorite. What does that mean?

Were you the prettiest?
Did you wear a red shawl?
Were your hands pushing him away
soft and warm on his skin?
Did you stare at him until he turned
and exchanged a human glance?
Was your beauty so perfect,
that like Beatrice, one glimpse of your face
could change a man's life?

Pale and frightened. That's how he described you.
A pale and frightened seventeen year old.
Your face comes to him everyday, Ina,
pale, frightened, alive, and his favorite.

THE JADE SUIT

A soldier digging trenches on Lingshan Mountain
breaks through crust and falls
through a tunnel strewn with rubble

into an underground palace muscled
out centuries ago
for the secret apartment of Prince Liu Sheng

bedchamber of Lady Dou Wan.
What the soldier touches turns
to dust. Silks, thin as locusts wings,

embroidered with scudding clouds, fill
his nostrils, coat his throat.
Yet the soldier thinks nothing

of these fancies, nothing of Liu Sheng's mantle
of terminal incorruptibility: two thousand green
squares sewn with gold thread, cool

as a chrysalis. He thinks instead
of green onions sending up shoots,
his mother slicing medallions

of bamboo the color of mutton-fat jade
his wife plopping a raspberry
nipple into his daughter's mouth

opened like a pale purple orchid.

Mnemosyne In The Garden
For Nancy Gotthart

Even the landscape fades
like the old photo you found
at the Chelsea flea market.

What's left of the silver salts
shows a tall woman, head
tilted to listen for wind, mouth

set in the half-smile of a stoic
who hasn't quite lost hope.
In the garden she can't leave

the stain of decay eats away
the trunk of the tree and the leaves
rusty as faded flowers found

in a mummy's tomb or as the small chunk
of stone from the walls of Carthage
saved in her cedar memory box.

SCARLET TANAGER
for Quinton Duval, 1948–2010

On the computer screen,
I study him, black-winged,
red bodied, in his sharp suit.

I click on the audio bar to hear his song —
cheerio cheer, chick burr, chick burr —
a song never heard in the west.

Spring is when the red bird sings, high
in the forests of the east — *cheer, cheer* —
to lure his shy olive-gray mate.

Here, on a clear November day
in the west, jays call and crows cry.
Sixty-two springs Quinton sang

his one long love song.
Now we tilt our ears to the sky
longing to hear his song again.

Elegy In The Old City Cemetery
for *Annie Menebroker, 1936–2016*

A new paradigm for the mind holds
it is like a cloud, vaporous, amorphous,
a shape-shifting function of imagination.

At the cemetery we eat brie and ham,
drink Chinese oolong in Japanese cups
of porcelain clay glazed matte black.

We talk of mood swings, mysterious dreams
of dying animals, cops and pilots who see
UFOs in the night desert sky at Roswell.

You drop your cup on cement. We see
it's bone white insides, a jagged break,
unmendable, even with gold. For solace

we construct a puffy white cumulus cloud
the kind children draw over tree tops
under the sun in a scribbled blue sky, ask

why, if the mind is a cloud we only imagine,
do we hold it so close like a friend
who's been given a death sentence?

Our breath displaces cold air here
in the graveyard where we picnic in winter,
condenses on the steps of a small mausoleum.

We press our noses to its milky glass door
like children shut out of their houses
on rainy days when no one is home.

THE NEW WORLD
after an etching by Sheila Sullivan

A pyramid, a chihuahua, and a woman
float over the table where, seated
the sanguine guests wait to see
the new world. Or are they
the new world, these people
who gather, hands folded, at the banquet?

And who is the hostess?
Is it the thin woman hovering over
the heads of the people who wait
to break bread at the table
in the miraculous world where
they are perpetual guests?

A raw-boned man (the guest speaker?)
rests sharp elbows on the table
surveying the strange world spread out
before him like a woman whose body
is the table of his desires. Meanwhile,
the people do all the things people do

when they are guests. They admire
the dishes set on the table, cluck
over the delicacies prepared, cast
grateful glances at the woman
who has invited them into her world.
Indeed, they think, this is

a new world and we are the lucky people
that generous woman has chosen
to be the first guests. The chihuahua
settles down in the middle of the table,
the *piece de resistance,* licking his lips.
Why aren't you eating?

the world weary woman complains.
*What kind of guests refuse to eat
the body of the host?* she sighs,
lamenting the work she has gone to.
Slowly, very slowly, the people
begin to eat the new world.

THE CLOCKMAKER: PIERRE JACQUET-DROZ

Poor Papa Jacquet-Droz
built himself two clock-work kids
and a wife of wood and brass.
The clever children made his fortune at court.
One could write, but could not read;
the other could draw, but could not see.
Yet ordered to make a portrait of Louis,
he deftly drew a small dog. His brother,
bent studiously over the escritoire wrote:
Any study of science is good.

But the woman, Marianne, pleased Papa the most.
She was made to curtsy and play compositions
of his own in the Italian style on a small organ.
He loved to watch her perfect breast rise and fall.
She could stay that way two hours at a stretch
and then sit quietly until he needed her again.

Together they watched the children play
or sat by the window watching the mechanical duck
preen his feathers, leave realistic droppings on the lawn,
and sometimes he muttered – that rational god,
that clockmaker Papa – how the first Marianne died
wearing her perishable flesh, bearing a noisy bit
of a thing who followed her mother's path.
These new children, now, helped out with the business.

Papa couldn't keep the orders filled,
though things dropped off a bit
after the Inquisition questioned
the maker of toy boys.

On long winter nights, snowflakes
falling outside the window, cogs spread
out on the table where the stilled duck sat,
firelight reflected in brass arms and legs,
the woman's breast rising and falling
slower and slower,it seemed, Papa flung
odorless droppings on the fire and cried:
Marianne, Marianne, ma femme.

VIOLA WEINBERG

Viola Weinberg is Sacramento Poet Laureate Emerita, serving from 2000-2002. She has published 10 books of poetry and a text on child abuse. Viola's work has appeared in numerous anthologies, journals, newspapers, magazines and online publications. She has contributed work to plays and musical compositions. For several years, she ran the Poetry Showcase for the San Francisco Bay Area Book Festival. In 2008, she was named the Glenna Luschei Distinguished Poet. She was also a recipient of the Mayor and Supervisors Award for the Arts in Sacramento.

Viola taught at CSU Sacramento, where she co-founded Women's Studies. She has worked in commercial and public media, including CPB and PBS. Viola moved back into publications at Mother Jones Magazine, where she was the founding Director of the International Fund for Documentary Photography, now housed in the Leica Foundation. For years, she served in an international brain trust for the C.S. Fund on social issues.

For the last 5 years, Viola has been fighting Stage Four cancer with hopeful results. She is the founder of the Tough Old Broads. Viola lives in rural Sonoma County with her husband, photographer Peter Spencer, and writes in a yurt.

I WILL NOT MISS THESE BAD WALLS
(for Peter with love)

With this terrible vinyl paper
spread lumpy, deteriorated
made to look like a formic potato
without the benefit of starch
impossible to lean on, punitive
with patterns of angry insects

I will not miss the jigsaw puzzle
with the missing pieces, spread
like a rash across a tiny table
irises done over and over then put away
forgotten and pulled out of the drawer
I will not bear it anymore

I will not miss the silent way
the waif janitress hangs
her enormous arachnid head
with those heroin varicose veins
and arms, a chicken rib's width
I will not miss the idle chatter
of lazy secretaries who ignore the sick

Or the tardiness of doctors
or the crate of pills to sort
some days more accurately than others
I will not miss the questions unanswered
or the gripping fear of earthly loss
or the brave bluing that fails to brighten

They say this is a place of healing
Better put, this is a place where parts
are lost and scars cultivate and lumpy
tumors grow, are poisoned and retreat
It is a sarcophagus shellacked with toxins
Some will live, and some go so quickly

I will not miss the fine fuzz
of lost hair, the soft stubble of grief
the maddening passivity of defeat in some
the trouncing determination of others
and always, the cheerful face I can't wait
to peel like an orange so I am real as before

I will be happy to reclaim my love
and his joyful, change-jangling electricity –
how his eyes shine with discoveries
I wait eagerly for the first laugh
that will erupt like a mud pot bubble
the way he heaves with a silent grin

I look forward to the reanimation
the warming of limbs, the settling
of his filmy digestion, the retreat
of his haze, O soon, please, his first morning
when we really know we are the lucky ones
the first flinging of his arms around me

I will wash him again, without the tubes
I will love him delicately until exuberance
tingles and a heartbeat samba begins again
With a flourish, I will show him the tiny bird
in the new red maple tree, the patient bird
who waited all this time for spring

DOWN AT THE MEXICAN GRAVEYARD

They are throwing a party with bass guitars
everywhere in the Mexican cemetery
tombs lined with the lost and the living
acrobats under a disco lamp that
throws stars, while widows mad
from grief 20 years now, rock, rock
on the spindle of their folding chairs
and sing like a shadow in the blue light
huddled and smoking, they languish
in the heavily scented imagination
endless rafts of sugar skulls

By this virtue, I should be standing
in the garden tonight, candles lit on
the sunflower bed in a deep row
I should be out there tonight, with my
anger and romance, in love and tatter
I should be howling at the moon, growling
breaking my fountain pen on the ground,
tearing the last of the blackened Giants of Russia
and African Possum Faces from her grip
in the earth, I should be smoking a cigar
in a negligee and talking to the sunflowers

Dissolute, holding a Scotch and milk – instead –
knocking back from the unspeakable madness
I can't stop talking about, waiting for night
to fall on the stoop of my shoulders, a hoarfrost
wounded, hateful and angry, wishing with
all I have for a Mariachi band in the summer
moonlight, blue as the grieving dresses of widows
Dignified street mutts poised on the monuments
the women drunk with pain and fury, gone, all gone
the planets whirling, each one a spent soul, drunk
as skunks and smoking like a barn afire

IN THAT STATE BETWEEN

The moment you hoisted yourself
on your elbows and the moment you cleared
your throat, while the orchid soaked in the sink
and the dog slept, late afternoon

Springtime arrived, unexpectedly glorious
accompanied by the ringing of bees returned
miraculously, industriously come back
despite dire predictions and a dank winter

They buzz outside a window on the staff
of the blood red rose that boasts a flower broad
as an old Italian summer hat with a green ribbon
made of sleepy souls and sweaty chests and half dreams

On pale blue sheets after lunch
while the daisy waits to be planted and a barrow
of rose petals dries in the sun, a small bird
stopped to peck at the dirt and a guitar played softly

Oh, the state between, when it's unclear
if we are alive or ascended, whether the stubborn Iris
blooming late against the green hydrangea is for real or
a painting of beautiful persistence, titled and torn

When the apple tree shakes her leaves in the warm
breezy air and two little songs seep from a hankering heart
The dog shakes his ears, gets a drink and
magically, the spell is gone

BEWARE THE LAMBS

In Scotland, I hiked through a sterile forest
along the Highlands, going west, frozen
Misplaced of time, me, an unfound mortal object
stopping in a dead village of crumbling stone
a village emptied, souls forced to factories years before
hungry ghosts gathered with me, unfurled, gone missing —

Back to that field of home in a forecast thick
with age, the storm of forgetting and the forgotten
the trial of wet, sticking truth with no coherent path
Along the way, a crude sign, old dripping paint
Beware the Lambs that stopped me cold
Everything in my heart died, my brain
and so much more in that instant with the lambs

I stopped to touch the stones and walk among them
I felt the disturbance, the force that took them
I can't remember the name of the forgotten village
or what they did, or how they dressed, I guessed
they drank tea that day, tea laced with, oh what was that?
It is the tea of the forgotten, the forgetting, the forgot

Vague childhoods, small rooms of darkness
the cool, quiet self-directed happiness of lambs
catalogs of unknown facts and blurry faces
children with wood, women at a fire, men
with the flock, walking meadow after meadow —
sudden shivering intense history unknown

Back in the present Highlands, I came across
an empty stone barn in that bitter gale
Inside, a skinned sheep with head hung from
the roof tree and I felt at home, so at home
It scared me, sent me out into the sleet
Thinking *the barn is what, that sheep is me*

CRAZY LOVE RAINS

It begins with a whimper
a storm sailing in from
another hemisphere, another pole
We never think it will amount to much

We don't know the fury of
that which is still unknown or
unimaginable, we think it will pass
easily, but it will pass like a gall stone

Slowly, with a buckling force we will never
understand, it will come creeping around
ugly as a monkey rumpus, we think we
will know what to do, but this is impossible

All our lives, we will underestimate
the bitter mental teas found in crazy love rains
Nasty stains of doing the same thing over and over
Foolish heroics, the ego thinks we can save what we love

Crazy love rains will snap like a sheet of thunder
We like the sound, even if it scares us
We think it's music, but really, it's thunder
Get out of the pool, and do it now, save yourself

Before you think you can withstand
the horrible electricity of a storm's
misunderstood fury, zig zagging dagger
Lay flat on the earth, spread out

Until you are a flat star in the dirt
until the clouds part and sun returns
Don't take it personally, don't go mad
don't raise your voice, just get up

with your broken heart and hank of hair
Don't think of how you once held it preciously
how downy it was in your grasp, the rosebud lips
Remember, it has the power to devour your liver and soul

PHOTO GENIUS
An Afternoon With Ansel Adams

We followed the trail of your hand
as you spoke, waving to the horizon
where a tiny ship plowed the water
a mere bubble on Earth's curve
"Imagine it," you said, "Imagine
a city of men, all working like dogs
maybe seeing the light bounce off
my window, at least one of them
is thinking, "Landfall!" you went on

And we followed you, working like dogs
Cameras clicking like old teeth
Motor-driven film and steel bodies
capturing images of the light, of us
but then it changed suddenly, resolutely
seemed to glower and burn, the sun
finally surged and fell flatly to the sea

"It's like that," you said, and
we all knew what you knew and what you meant
It was all about light crashing
geometrically on the back of a cloud —
jagged shadow, illuminating
the tiny hairs on the shivering cypress
as the wind blew icicles and night
tumbled in, rough and stark, papery
and sour yellow with grays in every range

A ship was coming in, in the dusky half-night —
inside, a fire threw our long shadows out to sea

Bonfire In A Blizzard

When I write, it's like a bonfire in a blizzard —
A red highway undulating in the desert
With my ancestors stuck, mouth down in the asphalt

And everything jerky and out of phase

Like at the movies when the projector jumps
Fast and nervous, almost out of the frame
And everything looks dead and pretty soon
You are talking to the dead with their black eyes
And pretty soon the dead are answering you
And suddenly, you look like the dead yourself
And you put on your little black hat and say

I'm a writer!

The blizzard in you lifts off like a rocket
And the stars blur, and you are thrown up
Into the next dimension at the speed of sound
By the sound of flight, like a baseball in flight
Flight through the dark, coming down hard and cold
You draw back your bat and wham! Home run!
And every blow you ever felt is released and

Your whole life flashes before you in one second
And every good thing you did looks good
And every bad thing you did is small and
All the dark poems you never finished finally go out
A particular run that burns black holes
In the journal where every stolen word resides

Wake up, Honey, Wake Up!

Writing is bleeding, blood draining from the hand
Ink seeping into the vein with capillary succulence
A small, illusional fire called passion, intensity, brilliance
Gravity will make your hands flap over your heart
Drawn magnetically by the force of every stinking word

LIGHT, THROUGH THE EYES
OF THE DEAD - FOR M.C.

A photograph, rich with grays
taken in a desecrated synagogue
Luminosity of debris and dirt
Rich detail of the foreground
O, the former majesty of you

I see it across the bookstore
So lush, so luminous and warm
I circle the rack like a tired flock of birds
that has unexpectedly found the roost,
shockingly white, molting and pink of eye

Into this book I fly to you, overjoyed
You, dead these long years, gone
and legendary to all the others
It all comes back – your scent, your laugh
the pearl of your eye under the lens

How I held the white cards
trudged with tripods and film bags
in the cold wind of the western sea
in the thin shelter of the small truck
with my heart pinned to yours

The greatness of the moment, private
and precious and famously expensive
You said not to worry so much
You promised to always be near
Now I clearly see through your eyes

Into that faceted chamber of love
into the next realm and through the last
your hands running over the large frame
the way your mouth formed the word "now"
I would hold my breath each time

Until the motor growled its click
and your face appeared again
the brown butter of your eyes
flashing dark eyelash and dimple
A black stone for the hole in a poet's head

BEDLAM

You saw me there
in the old city
not far from the wall
where old men
in little hats
and fringed shawls
tipped back and forth
laying tefellin
as they prayed for peace

The women come now
The brazen women
who stand and give forth
often with sour notes
to the dying and dead
Heads covered
Trying to be small
Hoping to be

Furiously
You called to me, "Help!"
you said, "They're taking me
from the medina to
the asylum;
They think
I'm sick or crazy
or crazy sick"

Your cloak was a sail
as you were transported
through Bethlehem's gates
The guards were gentle as monks
they knew you
and loved you as a colorful uncle
Wasn't the first time they had to
quiet the marketplace

Off to Bedlam,
the place disordered
You've been there
Carved out of dark sand
Bedlam sprung from insanity
Chaos reigned and the stone crumbled
If you are asked to join the pathos
your only chance is to face a wall and wail

EARLY MONDAY MORNING

And the carnies are packing up their
gaudy, neon-trimmed rides into
respectable wooden crates, numbered
in orderly sequence that fit nicely into
plywood gypsy wagons with words
like OCTOPUS and FUN and THRILLS
painted on the sides in drippy red flames
artistic little windows daubed on with curtains
a flower box there and more red geraniums

The DOME OF DOOM is disassembled
and SPIDER ISLAND is on its side
with its hummingbird tongue spokes
rising out of the dustry hardpan and weeds
Just last night, all the way to midnight
the greedy shucksters barked and wooed Rubes
as tiddlies winked at fools and their money
"Step right up, sucker," and step they did
Quarters flew from every pocket
onto the glass ashtrays in hope of a bear

In the harsh light of day at the stables, cowboys
are doing their laundry at the horse barns
Old blue shirts and denim dungarees flap
on rope lines, faded, seldom seen in open air
More than one caballero scrubs the horse blankets
and towels in a bucket to dry alongside the duds
One guy sits in a wheelchair as he pins up
the wet rags that curry a nag's sweaty hide
the cowboys will sit in the sun with a beer
and read the Bible while the carnies hurry ahead

Early Monday morning, and they drive on to Cottonwood
Later, the horse trainers will follow stitched to
their cowboy Cadillacs, hitched horses inside their
Hilton horse trailers with air conditioning and
mood music, as the carnies sweat inside old trucks ahead
The cowboy treasures — brushes, hoof trimmers and
ropes and bits — get packed for the next big Okie parade
puffing into the next county fair on a chance they might
run off with a bearded woman — who's having a thing
a fling with a sharpshooter in rawhide chaps
who sleeps in a tiger's cage down below.

I Taught The Boys To Dance

First, the painful box step, tracing
the square as if I were a plaza
where all the boys came to use
their left, heavy, size 11 clodhoppers
their lace-up Floorsheim boats
that crush a girl's thin leather

I didn't care, the boys didn't care
All an elaborate ruse to get next to a girl
An excuse to touch and steal a kiss
And still, I didn't much care, just knowing
that I could drive a boy mad was enough
Just knowing I could drop his hand

And walk away, easy as a grease slide
his sorry passions running after me
But then, I fell hard for a nice guy from Texas
a redhead and polite, who knew how to twirl me
do the UFO turn, a double-over-the-world move –
He had a way of snapping me like gum

People used to back away from us to gasp
My laugh was a gash of cherry red happiness
My heart was beating like a hammer on a horse shoe
tapping a maple tree in lost, distant snows
Suddenly, he had enough and left, walking
away with the secretly pregnant homecoming queen

Those who saw my shock briskly stepped up
to fling me through the Twist, the Cha Cha Cha
the Stroll, bouncing me through Be Bop
as that ballroom Lothario spun the queen, won her
in a simple plot of freckle-faced boy meets wrong girl
spinning her on a dance floor wet from a young poet's tears

His ring abruptly hung on another girl's chain;
I can't complain, my lucky heart was broken
for the first time, as I Jerked and Hully Gullied
angry as a bumble bee caught in a bottle
my sweeping curly hairdo unglued, and fell as
I hoofed it through the Pony and the Locomotion resumed

BEATING THE DEAD HORSE

For you, I will devise a canary
that fits in your mouth to be
covered by a black fishnet stocking
peeled down over your face making
your eyes ugly slits until they
run into your cheeks like diamonds
gone bad – your hands will be tied
to your feet with eels – your feet
will be tied to the eels with worms
The worms will come from Woolworth's
and your flesh will be smeared with
Rit Dye, not necessarily diluted but
Smashed all over like small pox
A long cord pulled from a box of
unbelievable torture instruments
will be pushed in one nostril and
pulled out the other – your sinuses
will be replaced by a pair of chickens
who are always molting – your teeth
will be transplanted to your ass
and you ass will be transplanted
to your forehead – I plan to rearrange
your thoughts and words and deeds around
the ass – Finally, finally, you will be
placed before a large neon sign – the pink
Day Glo kind – the one that blinks off and on
It never stops – it nearly blinds you
It always says, day or night:

I SHOULD HAVE LOVED HER BETTER
I SHOULD HAVE LOVED HER BETTER

LOVE AND WET SOCKS, THAT WEDNESDAY

When you knocked off early
when we were so tired, so weary
that we fell on the bed like the dead
Side by side, garden-dirty, the both of us
the soil and air both soft and warm
our tired feet in their wet socks hanging over the bed
toes cracking like castanets in the breeze

Too tired to talk, we just laid there, awake
you could hear appliances humming in the kitchen
you could hear the dog and his sloppy drinking
from the blue bowl, and a fly, a screen door somewhere
but, neither of us raised a finger, listening
instead to our beating hearts, those drums of blood
We simply let love wash over us, cleanse us

Heal us, peel the fatigue from our lives
Honeyed, loving thoughts were on our tongues
all the more sweet as time passed soundlessly
those minutes, so mute and beautiful are
somehow younger than the rest of our bodies
as if we threw away the infernal clock and calendar
cellular happiness, dwelling, abiding and deep

DEAR ANAIS

My clever, arching cat
You were not home
when I called, you were off
in Clichy with the degenerate
who has worn the "F" off
his typewriter as he fucks you
Forget his wretched mouth
I will exquisitely possess you with

A wandering pack of stars, roll you on
my tongue, as we create a perfect word —
I will play a Russian violin in
the verdant garden where I will bliss you
my slithery skin soft as cake frosting
then, I shall kiss the hem of your wet veil —
arouse the very god in you, O, come here!
I just couldn't wait, I have arrived first

In the teeming clover, smelling of basil
Carried by a summer swarm of bees from
the south, I've flown to Paris to
take you down, pluck you, taste you
my tiny, soft sparrow, run my hands
in your warm water as I tumble on you
luxuriously dividing the languid day with

A raft of pearl-tipped fingers that flash
in my grip as I pin you, feed you
bite-by-bite, cupping the stem with my teeth
until it is done and the dew of us stains
our mouths and our teeth are red
as berries, lipstick everywhere
our legs twisted in a pool of silk dresses
that stinks like the sop of a vixen kit

HOW TO PRAY IN KAZAKHSTAN
(Alma Ata, 1989)

Beware of dogs facing west
Horse skulls laid in moat
Beware the crystal breath caught
by paintings of the dead
and photographs that steal the soul
Remove your shoes at the door

Beware the tight, cold wire of false friends
on the high plain, beware of the steppes
that lead to the savanna, beware the
sleepy eyes of the Tien Shen Mountains
and the dangerous roar of spies who come to
hail and bury us deep in the ditch of glory

Beware of whistling indoors, but drink the tea
Beware of truths told in a woman's sleep
Be careful, please, to avoid the creaking trap
Step over the pit, walk the long way around
Share the sheep's eye, eat the cheek, stay
South of Siberia, the apples will make you complete

BEAUTIFUL

The way these stretch marks look –
the way their goat paths lead
to the red side of the monument
where the shape of my fluxgate measure
pounds like a great storm, beautiful
How they rush out like lightening
positively Byzantine the way they zig
and brand across the old continent
Beautiful, years later, after the rather
large-headed daughters with all the hair
split them first, dry as beach kindling –
Beautiful, how they grew wider
as I grew older, big as a steel storm door
and after, a toothpick in tight, high fashion and heels
then big again in love, and smaller again in pain
Years of inflatable/deflatable proclivity, beautiful
silver and white ribbons on belly and drumstick
dimpled Blue Plate mountains of distant history –
Beautiful, as the raw things that made them

A Memory Recovered While Deviling Eggs In The Delta

I was praying over deviled eggs in the heat of the day
shaving horseradish and mashing mustard and mayonnaise
placing little leaves of cilantro in jaunty patterns
and the whole mess – whites, yokes and all – in a Passover dish
It was hotter than the Galilee, sweat running, hair sticking
and I was at the counter, under the spell of Lucinda Williams

Singing 'C'mon now child, let's go for a ride'
and baby, for the first time in 30 years, I feel something good under me
like I'm behind the wheel of that sea foam green '55 Chevy Bel Air
with the big horses and the cool pipes and the accelerator
like a rough tongue on the open road ahead
Late at night on the Delta, my husband gone with his sax
somewhere where women dance in red dresses so

It's just me, with the two little girls in the backseat
asleep in seersucker pajamas with the windows down
cheeks aflame with the summer heat, the breeze up
Our way lit by an admiring moon as we drive on into the night
cutting through the Delta like a ship under swirling stars
or haystacks or fantastic whirling rotaries of old dreams

Going down like that, a cigarette burning in my ignorant lips
going down into the night, to meet my blue Venus
on the far horizon, rumbling toward Mercury and his message
too hot to turn on the radio, I let out an old Okie love song
faster than Sylvia Plath, back to those young cells of brunette rebellion
driving hard into the cradle of civilization, swinging in a wide Chevy

Tearing through the orchards down and up to the levee
unaware and uncaring if I would live to be 30
unknowing that I would go through men like cheap shoes
or that I was about to burn my bra or become a poet
just the black top river and beads of sweat on my neck and the coal
burning low and furious on my next-to-last cigarette

It was long before I knew about the future accountant
and the prospective human resources consultant
that would rise out of those two little girls in the back seat
I was 23 years old and they were all I had – and it felt good
to be flip as a cricket on the road, happily uninformed
about the books that were in me, or the long way back

I just kept driving, listening to the girls breathe quietly
in the summer heat and river breeze, happy as they could ever be
with their thumbs in their mouths and their stuffed bears
Their little feet tangled together, their lips crimson and full
with the smell of jasmine and pear blossoms to anoint us
The wing windows straight out to catch every inch of air

My pony-tailed hair flying with clouds of smoke
No idea of what would become of us or how hard it would be
No idea of the joy that waited for us, our many lives
fanned out in the hours of darkness that enfolded the future
No AC, just a bottle of frozen water on the seat
to roll on our brows and necks, summer in the West

Praying, like I pray over these egg yokes now –
thinking, 'please God, please don't ever let this road end.'

THE NEXT BIG ONE FROM TACOMA

Stands so white, his elbows folded like wet tissue
cheeks flaring scarlet in the blistering heat
a gawky monument high atop the 18" mound
a seven-foot beast from the Pacific Northwest

Stands like a derrick in Arabia, dunes shifting
his cold eyes pierce the little Dominican batter
with spare, mechanical flickers and naked
nineteen-year-old jitters on bony knuckles

Down on the plate, the batter looks terrified
the head of the bat drawn almost to his cheek
a tick visible from the bleachers, desperately
brave little man bares his teeth and waves his rear

Aw, come on Big One, you want me?
The Next Big One from Tacoma bursts
into the pitch, windmill and mitt and blade
It tears through the heavy air, born to rip

The guns behind the plate rear up and
the scouts clock the slingshot – 96 and flying
but it falls out of its screw, out of the trajectory
out of Big One's control and into little zurdo's zone

Wham! The Next Big One looks up
as the ball arcs over his high head, up over
his astonished eyes with their fluttering lids
Up! And, *O Dio Mio*, over the fence, he groans

The little batter, now a great hitter, runs the bases
His mother in the D.R. kneels in the church with her
hands knotted in prayer, feels sudden light and righteousness
just three cantos in, the jubilation tremolo like a weeping fan

TARANTELLA

A black velveteen river of tarantulas
coming down El Valle Grande, one
after another, the road eclipsed
cracking on our tires like eggs

Flying up the vents and smacking
the little metal doors, dear God
They were on the march and we
were in their way, as they tumbled

Creeping, a mob on the dark road
in a column on the asphalt as we
migrated bravely against the black tide
crunch on drang, a bad dream with

The foil of little freaky creatures
their insect fur and all their bright eyes
rimmed in brash sun, headed south
with their egg sacs and twitching limbs

Like Scorsese's eyebrows jumping at an idea
treacherous, disturbing, stomach-turning
We stubbornly drove against the grotesque
as they whirled, wheels of hairy little, tiny legs

Click-clacking against the windshield
and bumpers, the headlights and truck bed
We shouldered on, became angry, we sped
for 15 minutes in shivering tarnation until

We passed out of the storm, the sandy road ahead
clean as a beach, and we were quieted, but
even now, just the thought of it, the madness of it
will possess a stray hair to tickle us to death

IN THE NURSING HOME

A shriek rings out, a cry for
help like a dirty ring in the sink
Here, help me, I need to go home!
Soon, she is talking to herself

Bessie and Essie were twins!
Later, she admits, reluctantly
*Well, one was a baby and one
was a dog — or a baby cow*

Much later, about 3 a.m.
I need pain pills
My tortured leg feels like
a lobster bound in wire

I know it's here, somewhere
she cries as I take the second
pill and everything fades to a
deep rayon velvet shadow

I fall asleep thinking, one woman's
baby cow is another woman's baby
Some light filters through my roommate's
filmy curtain — out there, I think, out there

BEAUTIFUL SOLITUDE
for Monsieur Edw. Cahill of Montparnasse

There is no romance as rightful as that found, unbound
walking in a strange city in ringing silence, there is no
love greater than a poet falling in love with a place
where no one speaks her language and it's raining

I know the sultry nights, the marbled stones, the absinthe
of dreaming in beautiful solitude, the intoxication of gas lights
breathing evenly along a small street off the avenue where you
have penned a word with blood red lipstick on a matchbook

Taken from the drunken hand of a Russian sailor in a tiny
bar called Le Cave, where the vodka flows and everyone
is laughing, living and dying in the same breathless moment
and you don't feel beautiful, as much as wondrous and invincible

I know the sense of being utterly alone, as if in a womb
impenetrable, an unflinchable tower of the heart pulsing in you
a city that was always waiting for you, as if this city is your
true mother and not that poseur you remember from a spanking

This place never grows old in your imagination, or even
in a waking hour when the spirit of all you wished for as
a girl has faded, and a dirty floor calls your name or
when dinner, banal and inconsequential, is still uncooked

Trust me, this romance will outlast the miasmic linoleum of tattered
wishing although, by its very nature, it is mysteriously shellacked
by desire, because this city, this poem of your nature, this is more
honest than any impetuous promise or bond, this, *ma cheri*, is fact

Almost Him

I can still smell him, the curling ash
on a cigar he favored, something stolen
from his father, or his future, as we drank
from glasses of pilfered gin, sick as hounds
rolling on his bed, just short of it − all the while
wondering why we saved ourselves

And if we were really saving ourselves for
each other, or just mounting enough
sex and frustration to finally get to it
I couldn't imagine how it would be any different
from the mauling bears of breast-crushing
boys who always asked me to dance

How different they were from the sensitive poets
who recited the bard or went to Paris for a gap year
eventually proven gay, this being a theater town
with fests and feasts and a college that the town boys
never bothered with, resigning themselves to the mill
going direct to beer guts and shotguns and chaw

I used to wander alone through the park at night
decked out in my lacy gown, drinking from a
fountain that always ran, quietly barefoot and
full of grand Baroque ideas that seemed modest
under lamplight and moon, a Venice of the possible
an ache made of books and the dreamy great lagoon

A FAMILY OF WOMEN IN LOVE'S KITCHEN

Once while dining at the club
She went crazy, she stood and tore her
tailored linen blouse to shreds
The place was speechless
For a full minute the buttons flew
no silver stirred, no glass was raised

At other tables, other women
sat with their ankles crossed
in dresses of georgette and chiffon
They looked dimly into their plates
It was Sunday, Family Day at the club
but at our table, her big breasts

Were falling out of their white cups
and the harsh cry of a crow sputtered from her caw
bounced from the buffet table to the pool
Just as suddenly, she swept through
the room like a stately yacht –
Her flapping napkin flown low across the bow

NINETEEN ZIPPERS AND A DUCKTAIL

Nineteen zippers and a ducktail
High-waisted, skin-tight black pants
pegged at the ankle
embedded in white crew sox
blooming from the sex
of furry blue suede
needle-nosed brothel creepers

Small town tough guys
driving hiked up hot rods
Model T's and bulging Buicks
cut and torched and shined
decked in gaudy chrome hubcaps
whirling and whistling
in dangerous decoration
around the traffic light
right there on the
swaggering promenade
just before the high school gate

Late, slow talking boys
dipped in Dixie Peach Pomade
reeking of cheap cologne
A sparkling white tee shirt
creeping from the crannies
of greased up leather
ready for any kind of heavy weather
Nineteen zippers and a ducktail
Hot sweat slow dance breath-sucking
toilet paper flower-strewn gym
vague sweat sock stink blended
with toilet water and hairspray vapors

Corn starched can-can slips
sticky with board like texture
huge floozy-bells of cheap fashion
nineteen sixty-two
High on the power glide
of gas-swilling winged land yachts
with back seats big as the dull plains
of the rust belt from whence they emerged
soaked in sloe gin sticky as a flat Coke
Nineteen zippers and a ducktail
Spit curl shit-kicking winkle pickers
in dreamy late-night porch light
Hot tongue floating in the ear canal
A small pink boat of flesh

Elvis crooning on the radio
wrapped in pools of beery glow
Love me tender, love me true
Never let me go for my darling
I love you and I always will.

THE WORD WE DO NOT KNOW

I have been carving a poem from the pink flesh
Of an extinct, unpopular thought by using a word
I do not know — and every time, blood pops up
At the surface, as if in a dream where pieces of paper
can do what is drawn on them, perfectly.

I begin each morning beseechingly; I want it to be just right.
I am trying not to tell you the story, but let the image unfold.
It is hard, I tell you, old, the word we do not know.
I have been wanting to lay out that poem like a city
with an ancient forum at the center, next to the Two Widows

Of Roman stone that represent the distance and the future,
when what we do not know is revealed and then we know.
But the word clings to my palette like a mashed bean,
an ugly little landmark near Hangman's Bluff
where words are tortured and finally

Put out of their misery on greeting cards or in political speech,
and finally dangled as mangled nouns, now verbs.
I try, instead, to shape the word with my hands
preferring wet clay on a flying wheel —
wanting so badly for the poem to write itself

In the bold book and seraph of exquisite script
Godlike, impossible to conjugate or wrangle —
worshipped like a television set with 1,000 channels —
Not a synonym, nor a slow, second meaning
I give you the right word, the word we do not know

ON RALEY'S FIELD

A lush mown lawn lies green-on-green in tartan check
wrapped neatly on the shoulders of the mound —
white chalk ground along the lines, laced through long legs
of the luscious diamond where runners slide and fielders shield —

Abundant, verdant greens, dazzling and fresh, perfume of grass
with swollen, flat beads of dew on earth precisely groomed
white bags of base, white rubber of mound for pitcher's foot
and the precious place with spindled roof that we call home.

SALVADOR DALI TAKES HIS ANTEATER
FOR A STROLL IN PARIS, 1969

It was a day like any other in the Metro, Dali, waxed and oiled
His anteater smelling tarry and looking matted
The lady next to them sniffed and stood far away
The anteater was pleased, he disliked parfum and lavender

Dali was not thinking complicated thoughts
just trying to remember the words to
a simple Spanish song about a princess
a monkey and a coach with fine, golden ponies
The artist wiggled in his seat as the Metro lurched forward

Finally, they arrived at Avenue Émile Zola
allowing Dali and his anteater to exit
the first-class car where they always rode
away from the common riders, detached
by the necessity of the anteater's scent and Dali's claws

THIS IS AN OLD LOVE

Long since surrendered
strangely ample and triumphant
He scratches my back
I help him choose the green ink

I wasn't his first, or his first love
or even his second wife; I came at exactly
the right moment of the time of his life
I, who had ten recipes and 10,000 poems

Now wash his bottles, labor
over roast chickens and lavender
laugh at his bad jokes, fold his laundry
and castrate his detractors

WINTER COMES EARLY

Ice bedazzling on the roof
and the curl of wood smoke
from the chimney, the breath
Of a house the morning after
a hard freeze that left the
Bird-of-Paradise with a blanket
over its green, sharp leaves

I walk to the gate, crunching
a path that was quiet yesterday
The birds so happy then
are flying on, fleeing upper latitudes
and freezing tree limbs that wobble
as they launch, weary wings
beating the thick and thin air

Nothing is quiet this morning
Stubborn Venus on the horizon
Faint starlight frozen in space
Dawn's light cutting through
the frosted luminosity
A frozen pond glows with it —
the etched mirror of all we see

Xing Xing, The Stars

It is the dark of night in this lost village
I rise against you, a flag of flesh on your hand
the sky is moaning, nothing looks the same

Xing, Xing, the stars beam down on us
dangling white lights on beautiful ribbons
pinned to the small whiff of clouds

Caught in the Chinese tallow tree
Xing Xing, the stars come down to us
guiding our every move, providing light

As we bravely sail our ship above
an ignorant river of darkness
that only luminous love can light

Xing Xing, the stars
have put your lips to mine
in the watermarked taffeta sky

On the silk barge of the bed
lit up by Xing Xing the stars that
have brought us back from the dead

To love again on a moonless night
for life's energy and inevitability
drinking and breathing Xing Xing, the stars

ARTHUR'S SEAT, THE EASY WAY

It came in a dream, the sense of cold sunshine
The very blink of sweat on my fingers
I had done it before, trained for a year
Tore up the little mountain, the volcanic plug

Then I woke, and the dream woke with me
To find myself on my bonny, wee mountain again
To climb where I had climbed before the troubles
Before the cancer, before the titanium rods, the steel

I peeled myself from the sheets and began to train
I threw myself into the very muscle of desire
I wanted this with all I had, lumping up streets
And on to the park day-by-day, until I could

Fling myself up the dam bank and up to the path
Around the lake, where it was furiously hot
I didn't care, just flung myself through space
Clumsy as a kangaroo sewn to a chicken

Months later, Scotland nodded to me and I came –
I felt storied bravery, I prepared to climb up the easy side
The fervid beast of longing, I growled, I swore I would eat
That mountain, that I would win that mountain at 70

For mine was the battle of life over surrender
Mine was the fight of the century, I was not
Going home in limp failure, Mine was to crawl
To the top, to crow from the peak, taking it

There were those moments along the grassy side
When I panted how hard it was, how I didn't –
Just didn't know if I could go on, all the while
Shooting to the top, coming down blind with joy

The wet determination, the shoulders pushing
The face contorted, the absolutely grave fight
Inspiring those who followed, strangers, friends
Who stood aside to cry, "Braw victorie, Brave Lassie, braw!"

HELD TOGETHER

Laura Hohlwein
48" x 48" Oil on Canvas, 2017

PREVIOUSLY PUBLISHED WORK

ANNIE MENEBROKER

Composition - *The Measure of Small Gratitudes, 2011, Kamini Press*

Chrome Poem - *If You Are Creative, You Will Vanish, 1973*

Eddie Is A Doll Someone Sewed Together - *Dream Catcher, 1992*

In The River Town of Locke - *The Long Ride Home, 2016*

In The Soft Light of Being - *The Long Ride Home, 2016*

Love - *The Blue Fish, 1985*

Portrait At Dusk - *Watching From The Sky, 1989*

Remember Rita Hayworth - *first published, Medusa's Kitchen*

Singing The Bear Out Of The Woods - *Trying For The Ten Ring, 2000*

Something About Flying Pigs - *The Long Ride Home, 2016*

The Blue Fish - *The Blue Fish, 1985*

The Bull That Died In The Rain - *The Habit of Wishing, 1977*

The Oldest Profession (love) - *It Isn't Everything, 1968*

This - *Chiron Review, 1988*

Today It May Rain - *The Long Ride Home, 2016*

Very Small Slices - *The Long Ride Home, 2016*

Warming - *Small Crimes, 2008*

What It Is to Be a "Meat Poet" - *The Long Ride Home, 2016*

VIOLA WEINBERG

Down at the Mexican Graveyard, Beautiful Solitude
  - *poeticdiversity: the litzine of Los Angeles, 2014*

Salvador Dali Takes His Anteater for a Stroll in Paris, 1969
  - *poeticdiversity: the litzine of Los Angeles, 2017*

Arthur's Seat The Easy Way - *poeticdiversity, 2018*

Bonfire in a Blizzard, Bedlam, A Memory Recovered
  - *A Feast of the Will, Dog Skull Press, 2016*

In That State Between - *Art House America, 2014*

Beating the Dead Horse - *Scrambled Clams and Bananas, Woman's Organ Press, 1977*

Dear Anais - *The Four Chambered Heart: In Tribute To Anais Nin, Sybaritic Press, 2013*

The Next Big One from Tacoma, On Raley's Field
  - *Baseball Comes Home, Circus Catch Press, 2001*

Xing, Xing the Stars - *Public Monument, Sacramento, CA, 2006*

PREVIOUSLY PUBLISHED WORK

VICTORIA DALKEY

Chinoiserie - *Abraxas, 1983*

On the Seacoast of Bohemia, Charmin Billy - *Abraxas, 2007*

Mnemosyne in the Garden - *Abraxas, 2015*

Crows - *Cimarron Review, circa 1985–1985*

Pomegranate Seeds - *Divergent Lines, circa 1980–1981*

Odd Fellows Lawn - *Poet News, circa 1985*

Odd Fellows Lawn, Intersection: 34th and R - *In Lak'esh, 1991*

The Jade Suit, The Clockmaker: Pierre Jacquet-Droz - *Mockingbird, 1995*

Bonkei: A Model of the Delta (formerly "Bon Kei") - *Mindprint Review, circa 1978–1979*

Bonkei: A Model of the Delta (formerly "Bon Kei")
  - *Poems For All (Tough Old Broads Collection), 2016*

Reading a Used Book (formerly Reading A Used Book by John Crowe Ransom)
  - *Tule Review, 1998*

Reading a Used Book - *Poems For All, 2006*

The Yard Long Beans (formerly The Yardlong Beans") - *Watching From The Sky, 1985*

Listening to Bach's Double Concerto in D Minor (formerly "Listening to Bach's Double Concerto in G" sic), Easter Sunday, Pomegranate Seeds
  - *In the Absence of Silver (chapbook), 2005*

Chinoiserie, Crows, Pomegranate Seeds, Odd Fellows Lawn, Intersection: 34th and R, Bonkei: A Model of the Delta, The Jade Suit, The Clockmaker: Pierre Jacquet-Droz, Reading a Used Book, The Yard Long Beans - *twenty.nine poems (chapbook), 1999*

KATHRYN HOHLWEIN

In The Roanjin Garden - *Aufbruch In Die Mitteleren Jahre, Rowohlt of Hamburg*

Orchard XVI - *The Orchard Poems, Michigan Bar Press (chapbook)*

To St. Thomas Acquinas, Does God Ever Get Tired Of Moving
  In Mysterious Ways - *What's Funny About Forever, Random Lane Press*

TOUGH ENOUGH: Poems From The Tough Old Broads (first printing) is published in an edition of 300 copies.

Text: Body is Adobe Caslon Pro, 12pt leading 13.5pt stretched 125 percent horizontally. Poem headings are in Adobe Caslon Pro Caps, 14pt leading 18pt, stretched 135 percent horizontally. Page side headings are 9pt Adobe Caslon Pro, stretched 125 percent horizontally, printed with a fifty percent tint. Page numbers are 10pt Adobe Caslon Pro, condensed 85 percent horizontally, printed with a fifty percent tint.

Cover: Front Cover Illustration is by Laura Hohlwein (*Held Together*), modified by the artist for cover use. Book title is based on Adobe Garamond, modified, beveled and airbrushed. Small titles are in Adobe Garamond, stretched and airbrushed. Back Cover photographs are by Peter Spencer. Blurbs are Times New Roman, 10pt leading 12pt, stretched 125 percent horizontally. Cover design is by Bodhi.

Bio Photography: Inside Bio Photographs by Peter Spencer.

Paper: Interior pages are printed on 70# white 3.7 Caliper, 541 PPI. Soft Cover is printed on 12pt Cover stock 541 PPI and gloss laminated before binding.

Printing: This book was printed using Ricoh digital equipment.

Binding: Book is soft cover perfect bound.

Printed and bound by PG in the USA